UP FROM ADVERSITY

My Struggle for Survival

~

An Autobiography by

Joseph Beauchemin

12/27/06 Audrey & Tom

Once I couldn't spell Author, — Now I is one! Love Joe JB

PublishAmerica
Baltimore

First printing

At the specific preference of the author, PublishAmerica allowed this work to remain exactly as the author intended, verbatim, without editorial input.

ISBN: 1-4241-6092-8
PUBLISHED BY PUBLISHAMERICA, LLLP
www.publishamerica.com
Baltimore

Printed in the United States of America

Dedication

I am grateful to my daughter Tammy (Beauchemin) Johnson, who spent hours organizing the paragraphs and text of this book. Without her help and computer skills this book, "Up from Adversity" may never have been finished.

My wife Judy has continually supported my creativity and determination to complete the manuscript of this book. She has spent a great deal of time doing editing and proofreading. Thanks to her persistence and her loyalty toward the completion of this book, it became a reality.

Other Acknowledgments

Sister Gertrude Marie SSJ 1946 Eighth Grade Teacher - Her belief in me and her enjoyment of my stories, inspired a love of writing in me.

Along the way, Buck Riddell gave me a good suggestion for changing the title of the book to "Up from Adversity." Thank you. It stuck.

Thanks, Diane Hlad, for your moral support and friendship and to Marty Sherman for his computer expertise that helped so much.

I CAN DO ALL THINGS THROUGH CHRIST
WHO STRENGTHENS ME

Philippians 4:13

Table of Contents

Preface

This is a true story of my life and my struggle for survival against obstacles and adversities beyond my control.

This autobiography is a record of my efforts to cope and rise up from adversity and to gain the experience, knowledge and insights that would help me achieve survival and success.

At birth doctors predicted that I would not live to be 21 years old because of my defective heart valve (it would not close tight) allowing blood to leak back into the aortic heart valve chamber. In 1934 this condition was called "Leakage of the Heart." Because of the heart condition a very loud sound (murmur) was produced. Because of this, I suffered with a very limited amount of oxygenated blood supply to my body making it hard to build up muscle strength. Doctors wouldn't allow my participation in strenuous activities or competitive sports. I could not pass employment physicals. This made obtaining a living wage job to support myself and my family difficult. I learned to be a good salesman and so I got past the physical barriers and I became successful.

I've endured and overcome a multitude of life threatening traumas such as Scarlet Fever, Rheumatic Fever, Endocarditis, Congestive Heart Failure, two Open Heart Surgeries, Stroke, Major Chronic Depression, Seizures, Cellulitis, and many hospitalizations for other medical problems.

Some inspirational motivators that have helped me get through the struggle are:

"I can do ALL THINGS, Through CHRIST, Who STRENGTHENS ME."

"This is the day the Lord has made, let us be HAPPY in it"

"The Lord is my SHEPHERD; I shall NOT want"

"When FEAR knocks, answer with FAITH, and FEAR will DISAPPEAR!"

"What the MIND of man can CONCEIVE & BELIEVE, He can ACHIEVE."

Thanks to the blessings of my Lord Jesus Christ. I have survived to be 72 years old. The dedication and loyalty of my wife Judy gives me hope and enthusiasm for living each day.

My friends have suggested that I write down the experiences I've had in order to come up from adversity. Hopefully this may help others with their lives, because that was my purpose for writing and I hope it helps you. Thank you for reading.

Joseph Beauchemin, Author

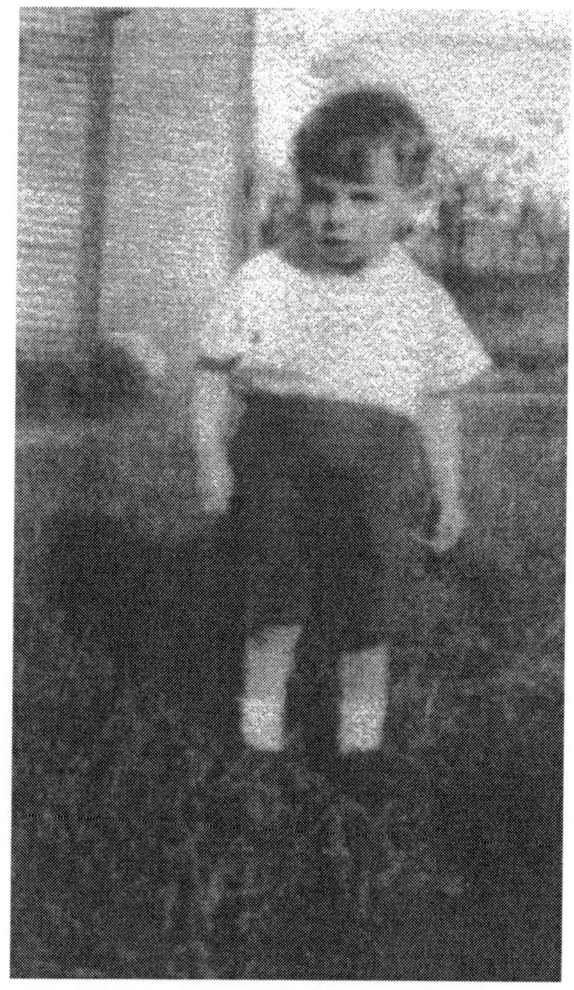

Me - Age 3: 1937

CHAPTER ONE
THE BEGINNING

My Family

Born 1934

Barrier (Gates) Family Homestead French Pioneer Settlement Rd, Moores Forks, NY.

The Beginning

It was a freezing, below zero winter night in Saranac Lake, New York. The day was February 24, 1934. Amid the birthing wails of my mother, I emerged into this world. Among the friendly Adirondack community, we were surrounded by the voices of relatives and friends congratulating my father that he now had a son. My mother held me lovingly in her arms and gave me the first nourishment of my life from her warm body. My proud parents were Oscar and Cecelia Beauchemin and they gave me the name of Edmund Joseph. I was named after my grandfather. They were happy, excited, and exhausted. They were being congratulated in both English and French since my parents were of French Canadian descent. Both languages were spoken at that time. There was sadness, however, that came over the place after the doctor had examined me. A loud thump, swish, thump beating sound came from my heart. It could be heard plainly without the aid of a stethoscope. I was born with a serious heart murmur from my aortic valve. A "leakage of the heart" was what the doctor told my mother. "The worst one I ever heard!" he continued. He even told my parents that he didn't believe I would live to be twenty one. This brought great sorrow to my gentle parents. It was the beginning of my greatest challenge. My struggle for survival was just starting.

My Father

My father was Oscar Leo Beauchemin (he pronounced it 'Bushman'). He was born August 26, 1907 in a little village called Standish in Clinton County, New York. His parents were Edmund (1874-1910) and Celina Royal Beauchemin (1877-1939). I never knew them. They had three boys and one girl. They were Edward, Raymond, Oscar, and Gladys. My Grandfather Edmund died at thirty six from a logging accident that crushed his head, while working in the woods. My Grandmother Celina suffered a nervous breakdown because of the shock of the death of Edmund. She couldn't or wouldn't raise their four children. She did recover later and she remarried and gave birth but she and the child died in childbirth. My father said that she was buried beside Grandfather Edmund in the Catholic Cemetery in Redford, New York, but there was no grave marker with her name. My Mom said that Dad often brought flowers to her grave.

After their death, Edward and Raymond went to live with and be raised by the Jesuit Fathers in Mount Assumption Institute in Plattsburgh, New York. Gladys was raised by her Aunt, with the last name of Otis, in Lake Clear, New York. My father, Oscar went to live with his Uncle Solomon and his Aunt Mabel Beauchemin in Saranac, Clinton County, New York. His Aunt Mabel was a teacher. He was never an adopted son. He grew up in Saranac on his Uncle's farm. In exchange for his room and board, etc., he worked on their dairy farm with a herd of 10-20 cows. My Dad was strong and had powerful hands from milking all those cows twice a day. Oscar attended Saranac School and graduated from high school. He told a story once about how he handled a bully who was picking on him. Clutching his lunch pail, he walked behind a tree waiting for the bully to pass. When the bully came by he popped him on the head and knocked him down and rendered him unconscious. My Father filled his lunch pail with cold water from a nearby brook and poured the water on to the bully's head to revive him. The bully didn't bother him anymore, in fact, they became good friends. My father's Aunt Mabel and Uncle Solomon were the nearest thing to parents for my father. They treated him well and he respected and appreciated them.

Dad at eighteen was well built and had thick black hair that he parted down the middle. That was 1923, and the "flapper" style and fad was in. He was very popular with the ladies. On dates and when he would go socializing, he usually dressed in a dark, double-breasted suit or tuxedo style suit with a white shirt and a bow tie and sometimes a dark felt hat or a French beret. He must have had a lot of girlfriends because of his good looks, personality and strength of character.

Despite the fact that his Aunt and Uncle would be unhappy about it, my father decided to leave the farm and be on his own. He discussed it with them. His uncle advised him, "You can leave if you are ready, however, if you do you'll have to be responsible for making your own living and have to take care of yourself. You won't be able to return to live with us again." My Father understood still he left the farm. He found a job that offered room and board plus wages. That took care of some of his problems. His job was that of kitchen helper and a dishwasher in a local TB Curing Cottage. This was about 1925 during the Great Depression. That was a big industry in the Adirondack economy in those days. Many of the homes had one or more open-air porches for use in the care of tuberculosis patients. The pure air was felt to contribute to a cure. Robert Louis Stevenson, the author, maintained a cottage in Saranac Lake to seek his cure from TB.

My father prospered very well in his new life style. He bought a new car, a Ford Whippet Coupe, in the newest body style, not the older rectangular body style. It had a 'rumble seat' in the back where a trunk usually was.

In 1929, the nation's depression period, medicine had advanced and there were new drugs that could treat TB better than the fresh air method. That meant an end of the TB Curing Cottage business and Dad's employment ceased. He would have to find a new job. He was now on his own. His pride would not let him consider the possibility of returning to live with his Uncle on the farm so he started to look for another job. During this time Saranac was just a small rural farm area and jobs were not to be found. He had heard of a business in Saranac Lake, the Gates Roofing Company that was hiring for their roofing business. He went to Saranac Lake. The Gates Roofing Company was owned by George Gates, brother of my mother. My Dad was hired and started working. Now he needed a place to stay and so Mr. Gates told him about a place that took in boarders. He roomed at Cecelia and Amelia's boarding home.

My Mother

My mother was Cecelia Gates Papineau (her first husband) Beauchemin. She was from a little town on the American/Canadian border called Mooers Forks in New York State. Her mother, and my

Grandmother, was Amelia Pare' Gates (1872-1955). She was short, at about five foot three and weighed about 100 pounds. She was feisty, energetic, and a hard working woman. Cecelia's father and my Grandfather was Felix Phillip Gates (Barrier in French means Gates). Nearest I could tell he died around 1933. He stood nearly seven feet tall and weighed about 250 pounds. He was a stone Mason by trade. He died of a ruptured appendix because he refused to have an operation. He was known to be normally gentle by nature. This was except when he was drunk; then he was quick tempered and mean. Once he was walking home drunk. A man blocked his path on the sidewalk and wouldn't yield way for him to pass. Felix got angry and punched the man, who died from the blow. The Sheriff ruled it was an accidental death…the victim just accidentally forgot who he was confronting. No charges were ever filed against Felix.

Amelia and Felix had two daughters, Cecelia and Della, and four sons Phillip, George, Leo, and Benjamin. In those days, "firebugs" were raiding farms and burning down barns. To be prepared to catch them when they struck, the rule was to keep a loaded shotgun hanging close by. Theirs was hanging from the rafters of the living room. One day the four boys were roughhousing in the living room when BANG! A terrifically loud shotgun blast was heard that shocked and frightened everyone in the house. When all the white smoke from the gunfire cleared out, a greater woe was revealed. Blood and gore was splattered all over the living room and on the boys. The violent jumping and roughhousing had knocked the shotgun off the rafters and it hit the floor and discharged, causing the tragedy. The load from the shotgun blast struck Benjamin in the head. The result was a ghastly beheading. His head was blown completely off. Amelia and Cecelia witnessed the tragedy and from that point on they both were deadly afraid of guns and were against keeping loaded or unloaded guns of any description in their houses ever again!

My mother was a good-looking, strong, stocky, pioneer type of woman. She had a wonderful sense of humor. She was very loyal, brave and protective of her loved ones. She was smart and a pretty girl in her youth. She was superstitious because of the times and environment in her life, but the paradox was that she was also very religious. She instilled in her children (Lillian, Joe, Ben) a strong faith in God and closeness with Him. Because her father had a misguided belief that girls didn't need schooling, her father wouldn't allow her to attend school to get educated. Therefore she never learned to read or write. When she was a young girl she had Polio and couldn't walk. Her father didn't believe she could be healed at the Brother Andrew Shrine in Montreal, Canada. Her local priest did and he took her there one day without her father's knowledge. She said that Brother Andrew was sitting at the top of a hill that had many steps leading up to where he was. He told her that if she wanted to be healed that she would have to come up the steps to where he was. She couldn't walk but had a strong faith and she managed to crawl all the way up to him. Then he told her, "Now you can walk back down...you are healed."

Even after she could walk her father still would not let her attend school. Just the same, she knew her "sums", was very smart and couldn't be cheated in making change. She was a wiz with her figures regarding money. She did all of the family's "trading" or shopping. She was an excellent cook and homemaker. She took in and did washing and ironing to earn extra money. She was a widow and had a daughter Ella Lillian Papineau (1929-1990).

After the death of Felix, I was told that the oldest son, Phillip sold the family house away from his mother and evicted her and the family. He then kept all the money for himself. George owned and operated Gates Roofing Company in Saranac Lake, with his brother Leo. My mother and my Grandmother who were both widows by then, decided to move to Saranac Lake, New York. They took in boarders and did other odd jobs to make a living. When Oscar, my father, moved to the area and started working at the roofing company, George told Oscar about their boarding house. He went there and rented a room. This is how my Dad and my mother met and started courting in the year 1932.

My Family

They courted until 1933 when they were wed. They were married in St. Bernard's Catholic Church in Saranac Lake. My father took on the responsibility and the support of a wife, a daughter, and a mother-in-law, but now he at last had a family of his own. The married couple, along with Amelia and Lillian, lived at 145 River Street on the corner of Slater Avenue in Saranac Lake, New York. My mother adored my father. He looked after her and made her happy and safe. They were an admirable married couple. They would be happy and together for 43 years until Dad died. They were great role models of a happy, successful marriage, for their children.

The next year, within those beautiful Adirondack Mountains, on February 24, 1934 I was born. A year after that on June 14, 1935 my brother Benjamin Anthony Beauchemin joined our family. His curly blonde hair was the envy of all the neighborhood girls. He was robust and healthy in all respects. Our little family unit was now complete: consisting of my father Oscar, my mother Cecelia, my grandmother Amelia, my sister Lillian, my brother Ben and myself. We were a wonderful and happy family.

CHAPTER TWO

THE EARLY YEARS

Childhood Memories

1934 - 1941

River Street Elementary School - across the street from 145 I went to first and second grade.

Early Years

As a young child I lived happily at 145 River Street in Saranac Lake, on the corner of Slater Avenue with my family. The house was across the street from the River Street Elementary School. For the first seven years of my life (1934-1941) I lived in this friendly environment. When I was an infant I fell off the porch and landed on my chest, hitting just above my heart. It left a big bruise and welt. Because of this and to protect me from more falls, my mother tied me to the end of a clothes line rope, when I was playing in the front yard. The house had an L shaped porch that had enough room under it for me to stand upright. I would use it as a hide out for play. The floor was dirt and I'd play there with toy soldiers.

My father was the best father a boy could have. He was a worthy role model for me. He was compassionate, strong, and gentle, highly respected and admired by his peers, coworkers, and especially by his family. I wanted him to be proud of me!

One of the first things that happened to our family was sometime around 1934. It is the story of my half-sister, Lillian when she was about five years old. Her father, Edmund Papineau, had died from Tuberculosis about a year before this incident.

One day Lillian was quietly playing with some stick matches that she found in the kitchen. She was fascinated by the fire that popped up when they were rubbed on the sidewalk. Being totally absorbed in her play, she didn't notice that fire had silently erupted into flames. It began hungrily consuming her clothes and had started biting into her tender flesh.

In her agony she screamed, "Help me! Somebody, please! I'm burning up!" The flames were completely enveloping her small body and could have burned her to ashes. Meanwhile, her mother paced back and forth hysterically, helpless; unable to stop the horrible scene she was witnessing that was killing her daughter.

"For the love of God can't anyone help her?" she called out and scanned the vicinity for a savior.

The only person who was nearby was Lillian's stepfather Oscar Beauchemin. He was hanging out the wash in the back of the house, where she was. He had presence of mind and acted fast. He grabbed up a nearby tub of wash water and drenched the girl by pouring it all over her. This helped to put out most of the flames, but some remained lingering in her clothes and he was afraid that they would start up again. So he tore off those smoldering clothes. When the clothes came off, pieces of charred skin came off also.

Her screams increased as the pain became unbearable. Searching for comfort, she cried out to her mother, "Mama…Mama!"

Her mother feared that the girl would die from the shock and trauma and she lifted her daughter up in her arms and hugged gently, all the while shedding large wet tears that dripped onto the little girl's body. The incident left horrible looking scars which she had for life that covered more than half of her body.

Even though this happen to Sister, (I always called her "Sister" and never called her by her real name) she appointed herself to be my guardian and mentor, always looking after me. She was five years older than me and scared away the bullies with her red hair, fierce temper and a million freckles. She had terrified them when she was mad. She would even physically beat off the bullies. We were close. By coping with her scars, she showed me how to handle adversity and to never give up. She had a great zest for life, was a true redhead and really something to deal with!

My mother was an excellent cook and homemaker. She took in and did washing and ironing to earn extra money. She took me with her to baby sit me while she worked. One day I saw the Goodyear Blimp fly overhead and not knowing what it was, I was terrified until my mother comforted me. Her ironing prowess was well known and sought after.

Easily, I can vividly remember Mama in her apron, tied around her, with the many handprints of flour when she made home baked breads, cakes and cookies. I was always rewarded with licking the bowls and spoons and can seem to taste that now. My favorite time was when she made batches of "fried cakes". All the neighborhood kids would gather around to get a sample. Then I was the most popular kid in town. There was no equal to my mother when it came to cooking or baking. The remarkable thing to me was that she had memorized all the recipes.

She was one of the most loving mothers that there ever was! It seems like I can still feel the warmth of her arms and lap, as she rocked me in the old rocking chair, no matter how big I got. She was a very hard worker, laboring to harvest fruit as a supplement to our family income. She did all her ironing with such care and concentration that the quality of her work became well known. She was sought after for her service to iron for wealthy women in town. They were happy to pay for her services.

My brother Benny liked to ride his tricycle on the sidewalk in front of the River Street School across the street from our house. Mom had a picture of him riding it there on the sidewalk. People would tell my mother what a pretty little girl she had. Ben would very strongly correct them saying, "I'm no girl!!...I'm a boy! "He started school at the normal age of five, but he was not mature enough to stay. In class he was fine until recess time. Then the teacher could not get him to go back to the classroom. He was held back for that year and had to start again the next year. He did well after that.

My Grandmother was always very energetic, a ball of fire. She always walked fast. In the winter she wore cleats on her shoes for safety on the ice. She called them her "creepers". She was devoted to Mary, God's mother and she was superstitious at the same time. She worked at St. Bernard's Catholic Church cleaning the church and replacing the burnt votive candles. The church seemed quite still and mysterious when there were no people attending mass. It also seemed spooky to me when I went along to help her. It would be later in life before I realized that her repeating the same French words over and over again was just her saying the Rosary. (She always said her prayers in French.)

She lived with us some of the time and sometimes with her sister-in-law Margaret Perry at her daughter Della Willette's in Saranac Lake. She shared a room, board, and a bed with my Aunt Margaret. Grandma used to keep crackers and goodies in her dresser drawer for snacks. She liked my visits and enjoyed when I had snacks with her in her room. She would always share them with me. It was nice to have her be there when I needed her help. She always preferred living with my Aunt Margaret at 46 Shepard Avenue over any place else.

My cousin Audrey Gates lived a few streets away. We used to go swimming in the little brook that flowed past our house. It had a gas smell and actually had gas streaks in it. We went swimming naked. It was all perfectly innocent, we were only kids. When my mother discovered us, she was embarrassed! She thought we would become the talk of the neighborhood and that it was a bad reflection on our moral upbringing.

I'll never forget the trick Audrey always played on poor, naive Cousin Joe (me). Whenever we had a game to play that required someone to be "it", she'd talk me into having a "Dead Man's Race" to see which of us would be "it". I would get all wound up and ready for the race. She would say, "Go!", and I would run as fast as I could. She wouldn't move a muscle. Then she would declare that I had to be "it" because I moved and that, "Dead men don't run!"

Audrey and my sister Lillian were about the same age, cousins, and good friends. They used to untie me from the leash rope that my mother had tied me on to keep me in the yard. Then they would take me on walks all over the neighborhood, then bring me back and tied me up again and leave me that way in the yard as if I had never left!

Childhood Memories

My first heartbreak came one day when I came home after school. My mother was not there to greet me. I was upset after searching and not finding her. I was crying and sitting on the front porch steps. I was heartbroken, thinking that my mother had left me! The Metropolitan Insurance Agent came by and saw me and tried to console me. He kept offering to give me a whole dollar bill if I would stop crying. My mom had only been upstairs visiting the neighbor. I stopped crying as soon as she appeared. He kept the dollar after all, but he was happy that I stopped crying.

One advantage of living on River Street was that all the kids that went to the River Street School parked their sleds in my front yard while they were in school. My best friend, Bobby Utting and I had our pick of sleds to use for the day, until the owners returned. Bobby was a little younger than me and he lived on my side of the street, two houses away. When I was about 4 years old (1938), I used to get up at daybreak and go wait on his back porch (playing with his many toys), until he woke up and his mother would let him come out to play. He had a Cocker Spaniel dog. My brother Ben came and tried to join in our play. We would sic the dog after him. Bobby's grandfather lived next door and had a nice crabapple tree in his front yard. We would climb up it and sit there eating the apples until we were full. Another one of our daily activities was to watch for the steam engine train as it came across the road. It came at the same time of day. After the train had gone by we would go down to the tracks and collect corks that would be left on the tracks. We never discovered who, why or where these corks came from but, there would always be some there. Bobby and I used to go to the movies most every Saturday. He would treat me, paying my ten cents for admission. They used to have door prize drawings at intermission that were exciting.

I would purposely get up before Dad went to work and get his lunch box. Pretending I was him, I would eat his sandwiches and goodies. He complained to Mom that he wasn't getting enough to eat in his lunch. She investigated and found me eating some of it. It was lucky for me that he had a sense of humor and laughed. Then he made me get the willow switch and he gave me a few raps. Boy, I had never believed that thing really worked! It did then!

At five years old I started school in the first grade in 1939 at the River Street School. The school was right across the street from my house. My first teacher was a Mrs. Starr. I learned to read and progressed very well. That Christmas I was chosen to play Santa Claus in our class play. Then Mrs. Starr got sick and a substitute teacher took over. That substitute teacher was worried about what might happen if I had heart problems during the play. She didn't want to handle the liability if that happened. She took me out of the play and replaced me. My self esteem was shattered. Disappointment turned to depression. I was heartbroken. Thankfully, my father came to my rescue. He took me out to buy ice cream and I was happy and accepted things, but never forgot.

I remember when I was five there was an incident that occurred regarding the pronunciation of my name. At a children's Christmas party the acting Santa was giving out presents to each child. He called for a Joseph 'BO-schema' and I didn't answer because I didn't know that he was calling me. My father told me to go get my present that Santa was calling me. I was confused and bewildered because my family always called me Joe 'Bushman'. This experience gave me strange feelings about who I really was. Was I adopted? Then my father explained the French pronunciation to me.

In Saranac Lake I made my "First Communion" in St. Bernard's Catholic Church. The Sacrament of First Confession was received prior to that. It was scary for a little kid like me. I remember being by myself, interrogated by the priest and being petrified walking home alone afterward. I don't remember why my mother wasn't with me. She usually was. I only had to walk a short distance to home. She met me there.

One day my father took me to a store where a pole with red and white stripes kept revolving. Dad called the man inside a barber, who placed a board across the arms of the chair and had me sit there while he covered me with a large cloth. With the humming sound of hair trimmers, he cut off my hair. This was my first hair cut. The barber complimented my dad on how well behaved I was. Dad stretched up to his full height in pride and he squared off his shoulders as he paid the barber for my haircut.

My family taught me to save my money. I saved it in a ceramic piggy bank. One afternoon I had wanted some candy. My family was all sitting together on the front porch on the other side of the house. Without asking my parents, I took some money out of my bank to go to the store for some candy. Not wanting to be seen by my family, I crawled out the open cellar window at the back of the house. Then I went across the street and through the cemetery, down behind the schoolhouse and across the street and dashed quickly into Mr.

Goodreau's Store. He was not surprised to see me there alone because I often came in to do an errand if I came for one of my neighbors. There I bought a bag full of penny candy and paid for it with the money from my bank. I said my quick goodbyes and then hustled to return home by the same zigzag route. I thought for sure that no one had seen me come or go. But, as I was crawling back through the cellar window that I had gone out by, what to my shaking limbs did appear, but my Dad with his switch and Mom with tears still in her eyes. I thought of offering them some candy but it didn't seem prudent. Dad showed me how a willow stick is really used. I never tried that stunt again!

My Aunt Deal (she preferred Della) and Uncle Phillip Willette were our closest relatives on my mother's side. They lived about ½ mile away, through a forest and up the side of a mountain. We had to take the path through the forest that led to their house. That walk was very scary. At the same time, it was an exciting adventure because of the dark, thick forest. My Father taught me how to collect the sap off a Spruce tree and chew it like chewing gum. It tasted good and was refreshing.

We often saw snakes. My mother taught me what to do if I came upon a snake. She said, "Don't ever try to out stare a snake! Snakes stare at you to mesmerize you. That's the way they catch birds." Most of the snakes where we lived were not poisonous. There is a big snake that is very common called an Adder or a milk snake because it is said that they suck the milk out of the udders of cows in the pasture.

My Aunt served a delicious meal while we were there. My Uncle's specialty was making home made ice cream for company who came to visit. The Willette's had 14 kids. That gave us plenty of people to play with.

Quite often in winter, temperatures were down to 40 degrees below zero. It was quite difficult to keep the house and ourselves warm. Most times the milk delivered to the porch was frozen in the bottle. One winter I got frost-bite on a finger on my right hand. It had to be lanced and the frost-bite removed. In order for us to stay warm one winter, all of us, my mother, grandmother, plus three of us kids had to get into the same bed and cover up, hoping to keep warm by our body heat.

My dad came home from work with $5.00, his work week's pay. He worked in the WPA government work program. One day he gave me a penny to spend at the store for some candy. The candy that I bought was all wrapped up and was sold as a surprise special. There was no way of knowing what was inside until it was bought and opened. Lucky me! Inside there was a nice piece of candy and a shiny new penny!

We liked to go to the store, with all its goodies, but we were short of money. One time, I spent most of the day trying to scrape the dairy's name off of a milk bottle so I could turn it in for 5 cents (only plain, unmarked bottles paid a refund). Luckily, the store owner took it and gave me the nickel!

I had the best times when my Dad took me fishing for bullheads in that beautiful oval Moody Pond. Once a big trout jumped out of the water and then splashed back in again. Dad said it was just getting its dinner.

Dad used to leave his car parked in the driveway. When he drove I would watch what he did. I thought I could drive a car too. Sure enough, I got the brake off and the car started to roll. Something didn't seem right! Dad stopped me after I had rolled out into the middle of the road. Oh boy! Here comes that willow switch again. He convinced me to wait until I got a little older before I drive.

One trip I remember when visiting my Aunt Mabel and Uncle Solomon in the Saranac valley. Dad had so many flat tires on the way there he had to end up driving the 30 miles back home on just the rims. My Uncle Leo brought Mom and the kids home to Saranac Lake. It took Dad many hours before he got home early the next morning.

I remember a house on Dorsey Avenue but I'm not sure whether I lived there or not, but I vividly remember that there was a nice lawn out back and a chain link fence along the bank of the raging Saranac River to keep kids safe and on the lawn side. Beyond the fence was a steep drop off on the edge of the river. As kids will do, we liked to crawl over the fence and throw rocks into the river. One day one of my playmates fell into the river when the bank collapsed under his weight. Thankfully his cries for help were answered by a neighbor man who scrambled down the bank and plunged into that cold mountain water. He managed to reach the child, but the swiftness of the water took both of them several yards downstream. Finally the river current pushed them toward shore. He managed to grasp an over hanging tree branch and pull them both out. Other neighbors helped get them to solid ground and safety. From then on no kid wanted to play rock throwing any more.

In the winter in Saranac Lake the town conducted a Winter Carnival Celebration with dog sled races, lumberjack competitions and ice skating demonstrations. The temperature sometimes dropped to 40 below zero which was ideal for the lake freezing with thick ice. Blocks of ice would be cut out of the lake ice and used as building blocks to build a big, fantastic ice castle. Then other ice that was cut out was to be stored in straw, in big barns, and used for refrigeration ice needs in the summer. It was interesting to watch the ice being cut out, as big toothed lumberjack saws were put into the lake water against the lake ice and the ice was sawed in blocks. Those blocks were used in building that beautiful palace. It is a fabulous sight, especially when lit from within.

Cigarettes were just 23 cents a pack then, but when they were sold in vending machines, they cost a quarter. There was a 2 cent rebate in the cellophane wrapper. I used to search through wastebaskets looking for pennies to spend.

At the beach in back of a big building of the NY National Guard headquarters, there was a small sandy beach where my dad taught us to swim. He always swam side stroke but he was a good swimmer.

Without closing my eyes I can visualize the places and people of my youthful days in Saranac Lake. All my life I have had strong emotional desires to return and live there again. No place else where I have been has been able to satisfy these longings from my heart. Partly it was comforting having so many relatives around. I was the happiest when I was there.

During the Depression I remember my Dad working as a Caddy on a golf course at Lake Placid Country Club seven miles away. He had to hitch-hike both ways to do it. Things were tough trying to support a family of five. He worked on WPA and CCA government programs where he took home only $5 for a full week's back-breaking work, but he kept us fed, clothed, and a roof over our heads. I remember him catching, cleaning, and peddling Bullheads in the neighborhood. He also spent hours picking, cleaning, and peddling berries. He probably didn't know that I observed him and knew that he did all this, but I did! The other work he did for extra cash was to dig graves. He was also enlisted in the local National Guard.

On Sunday, December 7th 1941, the Japanese attacked Pearl Harbor, Hawaii. That year was a sad one for me also, not just because of the war, but mostly because it was the year that we had to leave my most precious place, Saranac Lake. I remember the National Guard Unit mobilizing in reaction to the Japanese attack. Uniformed men were marching in formations, or hurrying to their assignments. For a young boy only seven years old, all the commotion and action were frightening. It also wetted my curiosity. Large, heavy tanks and troop trucks joined the local town's parade for a proud send off to the fathers, sons, and brothers marching off to war. My Father was classified 4-F by the Draft Board because of his bad flat feet. He had serious fallen arches. The worst flat feet, the Army doctors said, they had ever seen. That was the only reason he was rejected by the draft for service.

CHAPTER THREE

MOVE TO CANANDAIGUA

1941

Joe age seven

Dad always had to struggle to earn an adequate amount of money in our area to support our family. It became impossible for my father to earn enough income in Saranac Lake. My Uncle Oliver Pare' (Perry) had relocated to Canandaigua, N.Y. and he found good paying work at the VA Hospital there. He told my dad they were hiring and suggested he go there to see if he might get a job too. Dad took his advice. I believe that Dad must have had to sell his car for cash to pay travel expenses to go to Canandaigua. He was interviewed and got the job. He stayed with his brother Raymond temporarily. I remember wondering why he was leaving with his bags. I didn't know where he was going. He left home with his suitcase, and he was gone away for a terribly long time. He had to work for several months to save enough money to cover the cost of transportation fares to bring all of us to Canandaigua and to find a place for us to live. He only made about $25 bi-weekly. His performance and achievement on this has always been an example of his ability. He was a source of pride, as well as a role model for me. He continued to amaze me at how he could, twice every day, in good weather and bad, walk two miles each way to work at the hospital when he had such bad feet.

It was time to move away from Saranac Lake. Just like the soldiers we saw, we also were off with our gear and saying our goodbye's to our relatives, friends, and neighbors. Though this happened over sixty years ago, my memories stay alive and sharp because I have relived them over and over in my mind. I was motivated by a strong inner desire to be in Saranac Lake. The enticing aroma of Pine trees and wood smoke from home heating fires brought me warm nostalgic feelings, stirring my deepest emotions, bringing Saranac Lake back to my memory.

Leaving Saranac Lake

When finally the time had come for us to move to Canandaigua, my Father entrusted my mother to make all arrangements to gather us up and get us all on the train. Though I fought, cried, and screamed (I even hid way up under the front porch), I had no choice but to leave

Saranac Lake, all my cousins, and all my friends. Early in the morning my mother, Grandmother, her two cats (Tommy and Nancy), my sister Lillian, my brother Ben, and myself left our house in Saranac Lake and walked to the railroad train station and boarded a large iron monster that was pulled by a big steam engine. It blew a horn, spouted steam and smoke, and sounded like a dragon. It was fearfully noisy. This was the first time that any of us had ever ridden on a train.

Once we were on the train our fearfulness gave way to amazement and curiosity. The inside of the train held wonders that were new to us. First the conductor, in his black uniform, punching tickets with his shiny hole punch. Then the passengers in their city clothes, reading or having conversations. I sat next to the window and watched the Adirondack landscape roll by. I saw beautiful mountains, white clouds in the sky, and sometimes saw wildlife (like deer and rabbits) grazing in the meadows. Occasionally I would see a hobo shelter camp built in the woods beside the tracks. My brother Ben stared in disbelief at a seat that faced backwards. My sister Lillian, being the outgoing type, was annoying passengers asking many questions. Grandma was busy saying her Rosary. Mama brought her trusty bottle of Holy Water and was giving all of us a generous sprinkling.

In discussions with the conductor, Mama was gathering information and directions on what to do next on the way to our destination in Canandaigua. She found out that we had to change trains in Utica, then on to Syracuse where we had to change from train to greyhound bus for the last part of the trip before arriving in Canandaigua. I've always admired Mom's courage. She took on the responsibility of getting us safely through the trains and bus, when she couldn't even read or write. Mom was a simple mountain gal who never had gone farther away than 'next door' in her whole life and she had never ridden on a train or bus before either. I just found her to be amazing.

Once again Mama consulted with the train conductor to get information about which train we needed to take to continue our way to Syracuse. Utica was where we made the first change and got another the train for Syracuse. Utica was an underground terminal that was dark and scary. As our train continued, I became aware that the local landscape had changed. The land was flat and the mountains were gone. The thick green forest now became patches of hardwood trees, surrounded by rich farmland and crops. Instead of thick woods, it was mostly hedge rows. The atmosphere on the train was cold and unfriendly, not snug and happy like the mountains were.

We arrived at Syracuse and gathered our bags. The terminal where our train arrived was much brighter and thankfully at ground level. This was less depressing than the terminal at Utica. There were lots of people hurrying around. Some were carrying suitcases. Most were all dressed up in their city clothes. They were much fancier than our mountain people's clothes. Our conductor showed my mother where to meet the Greyhound bus.

To get the rest of the way to Canandaigua we had to board a Greyhound bus. That was less comfortable than the train. The driver had to make temporary stops frequently. The sky was overcast with big dark clouds. A storm was approaching as we moved west toward Canandaigua. Less than an hour into this part of the trip it started to rain. With unbelievably loud claps of thunder, the sky seemed to open up with the worst storm I had ever experienced. Lightening flashed menacingly and many trees were hit. Branches were strewn all over the edges of the road. The accompanying rain came down like Niagara Falls, and was threatening to flood the whole countryside. Then the rain changed to a hail storm with very strong winds. We were all very scared! At home Mama would have gotten out the "Holy Water" to sprinkle on us to protect us, so she got out the Holy Water now and sprinkled us good. The storm lasted all the rest of the way to Canandaigua.

We finally arrived safely in Canandaigua. It was dark when we reached town, even though it was only afternoon. There were tree branches and other debris scattered all over the roadside. Some large trees had been hit by lightening and blown down. It was the worst thunderstorm that the area had ever seen, so we were told. The Canandaigua Main street was made of yellow bricks that had been laid by Italian immigrants in the early 1900s. When we arrived there were several big potholes. I will never forget it. Trolley tracks ran up and down Main Street. Canandaigua was laid out like a western town. On each side of the street the sidewalks were twelve to fifteen feet wide. They sloped up the street through the town until they reached the railroad tracks. North Main Street continued beyond them for at least a half mile. The Court House was located on a rise, with several steps going up to it. The statue of justice holding a scale was mounted to the top of the Court House as a prominent landmark. Along each side of the street there were many gigantic Elm trees that were easily over one hundred years old. There were three story buildings on each side of the street. The air was damp and chilly. My first impulse was to plan a way to get out of this town and go back to the mountains. We were exhausted from our trip so we stayed that night with my Uncle Raymond and Cousin Audrey. The next day we would go to our new home on Main Street.

Dad (Oscar) and Mom (Ceil)

CHAPTER FOUR

GROWING UP IN CANANDAIGUA

1941 - 1951

Brother Ben - age 15

Joe - age 16 1950

Our New Home

Our new home was an apartment at 389 South Main Street, Canandaigua. It was an older, three family house. The Landlord lived in the small upstairs apartment with his wife. Their name was Robinson. They were a nice elderly couple. The downstairs apartment on the left was rented to the Craugh family. They had five or six kids. Our apartment was downstairs on the right. My family had two parents, a grandmother with two cats, my sister, my brother, and me. The house looked clean but the condition of the apartment was horrendous! The walls, ceiling, and floors were almost black from all the cockroaches crawling around. It was unbelievable! We had to start a new school in the morning and in order to get any sleep my Grandmother had to keep watch over us all night to keep those critters off of us. The next day my father and mother fumigated the whole apartment.

My sister Lillian, my brother Benny, and I had to start a new school in the morning. We started at St. Mary's Catholic School in 1941. We were taught by Nuns of St. Joseph's order. They wore habits of black and white. They were strict disciplinarians. For us this was quite a change from Public School. I started in the third grade, my brother Ben in the second, and my sister Lillian in the fifth grade. The school was on North Main Street behind the church. It was a half mile from our home. My Grandma's kitten, Tommy liked to follow me to school and wait for me to come home.

In the first winter the snow that was blown around by the fierce cold winds drifted five to eight feet high. The wind chill factor temperatures got as cold as 20 degrees below zero. We were used to living in cold weather and wore clothes suited for it. I was dressed in my bests, brand new clothes, what I called my "Mountain Style Clothes". I wore wool knickers (pants), with long brown stockings and a flannel shirt. In the Adirondack Mountains my outfit was very stylish and practical, where it can get as cold as 20 to 40 degrees below zero. The kids in school made nasty remarks about us and made fun of our clothes. Our names, Beauchemin and Papineau caused more ridicule and picking on. We got into many fights. Also our mountain accents gave them another thing to criticize. The Italian kids outnumbered us and they all had family or relatives nearby. The differences in our language and customs were hard to blend. It took a long time for them to befriend us, and us them. My sister Lillian would often break up the fights of bullies who would try to pick on me. They didn't want her angry with them so they would cooperate with her.

My sister Lillian could beat up any bullies that picked on me. She was five years older than me and had a fiery temper. My brother Ben was about a year younger than me. His personality was not compatible with mine most of the time. Though I loved him as a brother, we were not chums. Most of the kids attending school were either Italian or Irish and they all had plenty of siblings or relatives. But compared to them there was only my brother and sister and my cousin Audrey Gates. Back in the mountains we had lots of kin. I felt like a coward with one bully for not making him stop, but it seemed more prudent to let him keep chasing me as long as I wasn't caught. He was so much bigger than me! There were other bullies that gave me trouble too, like the two Irish brothers that punched me and wanted to have a fight with me. The older one started fighting first. When it looked as if I was winning and not giving up, then the youngest one started punching me too. He was supposed to be the referee to keep the fight from being a two on one battle. As they were punching I kept saying "Is that all the harder you can hit?" I backed away from them and insulted their prowess and told them I wouldn't fight with opponents who didn't have integrity. They stopped and considered what I had said to them, thought about it for awhile, then went home sheepishly.

I finally had enough of being bullied, but there was a group of Italian kids who had been chasing me home who planned on bullying me. I stopped running and made a fist and then put my arm out to the side in a stiff arm position. As the first bully went by me he ran into my fist and arm. He got knocked out! When the rest of the group saw what happened, they were stunned by my turn around and they quickly made a fast disappearance, making tracks for home. After that I didn't have any problems with bullies. That boy who got knocked out and I became good friends for over 60 years.

In order to get money to get out of that bad apartment, Mom took a job harvesting raspberries. She worked from six in the morning until six in the evening, working all day in the hot sun, bent over picking berries. With no babysitter, she had to take us three kids with her sometimes. We weren't much help to her though, because we weren't used to doing hard work and we were mostly lazy. After a year she was able to save money enough for us to rent a whole house that was for our family alone. The house she found us was at 109 Pleasant Street and we settled in to grow up in Canandaigua.

Growing Up

After we were settled in the Pleasant Street house we lived there and we were happy. Dad worked at the VA Hospital which was a half mile from our house. Dad didn't own a car in the first fifteen years and he walked to work and back home every day, no matter what the weather was like. I don't know how he could keep doing it, day after day? He was strong from all the farm work he had done as a boy, but was gentle and compassionate. That's why he did so well as a Nursing Assistant at the VA Hospital. He would work there for 35 years.

Surprisingly, my mother won a raffle at St. Mary's Church and won a brand new Dodge Sedan. She was so happy to be able to give it to my dad, who of course was extremely happy to have it. Dad worked the 3 pm to 11 pm shift. Before work he liked to swim and sun bathe at Kershaw Park. I'm sure he enjoyed seeing the women swimmers. Mom got dizzy easily and fainted from watching the movement of the water so she seldom went with him. We didn't see much of him, except days, because we were in bed when he got home from work. Mom's main role was wife and mother, but for one brief time during WWII she worked in a factory. She was pressured sexually by the males that worked in the factory and therefore she kept an ax handle on her work bench and wasn't shy about hitting someone over the head with it if she had to. One night she was brought home by workers after she had a dizzy spell. She had passed out at work. Thankfully she was not seriously hurt but after that Dad insisted that she quit the factory job. This was during the war and the wages from factory work were extremely good. They would miss the extra income, but her welfare was what was most important.

My Grandmother was very proud and very independent. One time she had a disagreement with Dad about something and got very upset. She was very angry with my father. She left our home and disappeared for a while. She was not in the best physical shape and she was 68 years old. My father and mother were very worried about her safety and whereabouts. She had been gone for a week. My Father searched everywhere for her and after some searching he found her working as a dishwasher in a restaurant. He discovered that she had moved in with a fellow worker from the restaurant where she was working. After some discussions, my Father (a softy) made up with her and she agreed to come back home if Dad would apologize, which he gladly did. He got her to come back to live at our house again. Grandma stayed with us for a short time. Most of the rest of her life she would live with her daughter, Della Willette at 46 Shepard Ave. in Saranac Lake. She shared a room and bed there with her sister-in-law Margaret Perry. She returned to us years later and died in the Canandaigua hospital from Sclerosis of the Liver, although she never drank liquor in her life.

Once I stayed up all night watching an enormous meteor shower. I had come from the Playhouse Theater in Canandaigua and was walking home. This was in the fall of 1946 and I was 12 years old. A bright falling star appeared in the sky. Then I noticed there were many other falling stars too. I became both frightened and curious at the same time. I hurried home to 109 Pleasant Street to my mother and sat on the front porch with her, watching the display in the sky. The rest of my family joined us for awhile and then they went to bed. I was spellbound and stayed up all night transfixed by the meteor display.

I have always loved to read. Unfortunately my sister abused the library rules and privileges and cost my father money in fines.

Because of this I was not allowed to take books out and bring them home to read. So I used to stop in at the library afternoons after school. Mostly I would read books that the librarian suggested to me. My favorites were: Katie Did It, a children's story series, Robin Hood, and The Indian How Book. I was fascinated with books about Indians, woodcraft and history. I read all the Lincoln series by Carl Sandburg. I have always tried to acquire and practice Lincoln's integrity and empathy, in my dealings with people.

I graduated from St. Mary's Catholic School in 1947. I passed the Regents exams for qualification to high school. In the Fall I started high school at the Canandaigua Academy in the class of 1951. I took courses in Industrial Arts. The school was about a mile from my home and I walked or rode my bike. I was allowed to take Gym but not competitive athletics. For spending money I mowed the lawn of one of my teachers. I also had a Daily Messenger paper route. In the evening I worked as a pinsetter at Adams Bowling Alley. I did these things when I was from 12 to 16 years old. At school I tried out for the school swim team and qualified for the team, but the doctors would not give their approval for me to compete. This made me feel inferior, depressed and spiritually disappointed. The restrictions that were placed on me because of my heart problem added to my depression and I lost all enthusiasm or motivation for continuing in school. I quit school at 16 years old when I was a senior. I found a job instead of graduating. Fate stepped in though, as I only worked for one day and then I was fired. Other employees, playing around, got the production line all jammed up. It stayed held up for more than an hour. The boss blamed me for it, though it was not my fault! Then I was too proud to register or re-enroll in that school again. So life took me on another path to adventures.

CHAPTER FIVE

ADVENTURES

1946 - 1950

Dad and I

When I was about 16, my father shared with me some of his experiences and adventures. He left me several pictures of himself, his car and some of his girlfriends. He never told me about the birds and bees directly, but he knew that I knew and also, I knew that he knew that I knew! What else was there to be said?

Dad liked to go to Kershaw Park to swim and relax in the sun. There is an island in Canandaigua Lake called Squaw Island that could be reached by wading from a spot where the Sucker Brook runs into the lake and makes sandbars to wade on. One day, I coaxed him to come camping with my brother Ben and I at this location. He dragged my wagon, packed with camping gear, down to this camping spot. He pitched a pup-tent, then we went swimming and wadded out to Squaw Island. We had a great time. He had a good sense of humor and liked to play. He spent some time again, teaching me how to swim. He swam using the breast stroke. When we came back to the tent expecting to go to bed, the inside of the tent was full of mosquito's swarming all over and biting us. Dad insisted that we pack up everything and he took us back home rather than to get bit all night.

Another adventure Dad took me on was a fishing trip with some of his friends from work. I was about 17. We went to Woodville, on Canandaigua Lake. They had their own boat and Dad rented a row boat for us and we started fishing in the lake. Wow, was that lake ever deep where we fished. I couldn't believe how much line it took to get down to where the fish were biting, about 300 feet. Dad rowed the boat while I fished. We went quite a ways up the West River outlet of Canandaigua Lake and back. We caught a few Perch, but otherwise the fishing was lousy. Still, I had a chance to enjoy my Dad's company and to observe what he was like away from home. He was completely different than he was at home! He sounded like he was at work talking to VA patients. He actually scared me and I didn't know him that way! I think it was his way of telling me about the birds and the bees. Anyway, it was a great day being with him.

Boy Scouts 1948

Between 1946 and 1951 I was very active in our Boy Scout Troup #33 in Canandaigua. Back then, one had to qualify in order to join the Scouts. My test was to be able to travel one mile in a certain time limit, using the Scout's pace that combined running and fast walking. With my heart murmur, it was very doubtful that I could go the distance. With the whole gang of boys cheering me on and with blurred vision and pounding heart, I qualified just in the knick of the time allowed. Camping and sleeping outdoors were some of my favorite activities. My motivation as a Scout came from treating my membership as if I were in the military. I practiced disciplining myself and keeping myself physically and mentally fit and observing Scout oaths and laws. I later became a Cub Scout Den Chief and Jr. Assistant Scout Master.

I was selected to represent our troop at the 1950 Boy Scout Jamboree at Valley Forge, Pa., but I was not allowed to attend because of my heart murmur. No doctor would give the approval for my going. That was another of those bitter disappointments in my life. Fatefully, it turned out that there was a Polio epidemic that broke out at the Jamboree that year, so it was good that I did not go.

We really enjoyed using our bicycles. On weekends we would pack all our camping gear on to our bikes and go on long rides for camping. Our favorite spot was seven miles out the West Lake Road of Canandaigua Lake. Along the way and about five miles out there is a very steep hill. We called this point the first Menteeth. Going over the top of the hill there was the first landmark, a religious, shrine-like statuary of the Sacred Heart of Jesus. A quarter of a mile farther on was a big farm where turkeys were raised. Whenever we rode by we would call to the turkeys and get them making a loud gobbling noise. A little farther on we met the last big hill. It was at least a half mile down hill and brought us to the second Menteeth Point, which was our destination for camping. There is a gully there with a gorgeous waterfall and a good sized pool of water enticing us at the base of the falls. We spent many nights camping nearby and went swimming in that pool of cold water. There was a big white Tavern that had been a Stagecoach House. In the back there was a

Carriage House about 8 feet wide and about 15 feet long with a dirt floor. This is where we camped out many times. One night, the boy who was supposed to camp overnight with me had second thoughts and got cold feet and he went back home. That left me to stay overnight by myself. It was a little scary, but I stuck to it and stayed the night safely. In the morning I had to pack up the gear of both of us and get it to the roadside, bikes and all. Finally, I was able to get a ride home in a car by a nice lady who felt sorry for me.

On another bike trip to Menteeth, one of my friends had an accident as we rode our bikes back home. Coming down the ½ mile steep hill at the first Menteeth, we were all showing off by riding down the hill without holding onto our bike with our hands. The bikes started to shimmy and this one boy lost control. His bike tipped over and he was dragged all the way down the hill. He was skinned badly and a few cuts were bleeding. The largest, strongest boy in our group, Barney put the boy on the handlebars and he peddled him on his bike all the way to the hospital for medical treatment in Canandaigua, seven miles away.

Another bike trip ended in a more humorous way. My friend and I skipped school one day to go to Menteeth. We had just started riding up the West Lake Road, when a terrible thunder and lightening storm began. We then were showered with hail stones that were the size of moth balls. Honest! We needed shelter in a hurry. There was a man working in his garage tending to the baby chicks he was raising. It was dry, safe and warm there, so we appealed to him for shelter, which he gladly obliged. We decided to wait there until the end of the storm before trying to go on. Just then his wife drove up in her car. You will never guess who his wife was. We knew our fates were sealed. The wife was the Truant Officer! She lived there! Can you believe that! She took us back to school immediately.

One time, while working on earning a Camping Merit Badge in Scouts. My friend Judson Ingraham and I teamed up to work on earning it. We had to do several specific types of camping. The first type was camping with no matches, using only flint and steel. We selected a camping site that was as far away from civilization as we could, somewhere off the West Lake Road. For shelter, we set up the

Army Surplus Shelter-Half Tent my father had bought me. Then we prepared for our evening meal. To use flint and steel to start a fire, it is important to have a proper fire foundation to catch the spark. I laid down a bed of dried grass and on top of that I laid a charred cloth to catch the spark. By striking the steel against the flint a spark was produced and it landed on the charred cloth and stayed alive long enough to pick the tinder up and blow the spark into a flame. Once the flame was produced then I laid dry branches (I call squaw wood), on the sticks in the fashion of a tepee. Once the tepee burned down to hot coals, then I crisscrossed sticks of larger size on the hot coals. I didn't want a big flaming fire, like a tenderfoot's. It's the hot coals that are best for cooking. Jud was an excellent cook and he soon had fixed us a great camp meal.

After supper we decided to go to bed because it had started to rain and some thunder could be heard. I woke up in the night smelling a strong odor. I turned on my flashlight to see where the odor was coming from. There at the foot of our bedrolls, in the cover of the front tent flap was a large black and white skunk, sleeping soundly. I woke Jud up carefully and quietly and told him to see our guest. We agreed that the only thing to do was to sleep as still as we could and hope it would be gone in the morning. Thankfully, he was gone, but his fragrance wasn't!

Another time, we were trying to camp for a whole week without having to come back to civilization. Jud and I hiked up the gorge of the first Menteeth (about five miles up the West Lake Road on Canandaigua Lake). We hiked through a forest of young pines and tall, broad Maple and Oak trees. We found an ideal campsite with a clear running brook passing through a small clearing. A small wall tent that we borrowed from our scout troop made an ideal home for us to stay in for a week of camping. We made two beds (side by side) and then piled three to five inches of fallen pines needles in each bed site. We spread ground-cloths before putting down the sleeping bags where depressions were scooped out for where our hips and shoulders would lay against the ground. To be prepared should it rain, a channel was made around three sides of the tent and a ditch to drain water off and away from the bottom of the tent. For cooking fire, I dug a trench about three feet long and found a couple of large flat rocks to set hot pans on. That completed our kitchen. Then our camp was ready. We gathered up sticks and tinder to save for making a fire. Just beyond the cook fire trench we made a circle of large round stones to make a campfire circle and dug a hole in the center. Lastly, I gathered up logs to use for a camp-fire. Now our camp was ready, snug and prepared. Jud cooked a good super at this camp too and we ate our fill.

One day I had gone to town for supplies and I had just returned to our camp. At first I could not believe what I saw. A man dressed in buckskin clothes carrying a Revolutionary War flint lock rifle, stood by the tent. Over his shoulder hung a bag of lead shot and powder horn. He spotted me trying to sneak back to camp without being seen. He came walking toward me, looking straight at me. I had no idea what fate awaited me. I was relieved when he turned out to be a friend. He was the son of the man who owned the property we were camping on. He was a collector of Early American firearms. He liked to hunt for woodchucks where we were, using one of his black powder rifles. He invited us to come with him, but we declined and thanked him for letting us camp on his land.

Neighborhood

Some of the games we played in our neighborhood were, Capture the Flag and playing Tag on the rooftops of stores on Main Street. One night the Alley Cop (policeman) caught us on the roof tops. He gathered us in a group and was preparing to take us to the Police Station when one of the guys bolted and ran away. That Cop got nervous and drew his gun and called to the boy to stop. He didn't and the Cop was leveling his gun, preparing to shoot, when the boy turned a corner and was gone. Later, about half-way to the Police Station, that boy caught up with us saying that he only ran because someone called him a name. He thought he better join up with the Cop or it would go bad for him. We were given a stern lecture then released swearing never to let him catch us doing that again. He never did.

"Donkey on the Can" was a game we played most every night in the summer in our neighborhood. All players have a can. The one who is "it" sets his can in the middle of a circle on the ground, as his goal. Everyone else runs and hides. The one who is "it" searches for the others. They try to get to the goal to knock down "it's" can with their can, before they were caught. If they get caught they are out of the game until some other player can knock the can down. With that everyone who was caught before is free and the game starts over again. We would holler "Don't be a goal sticker!" to get "it" to come after us. The game is a combination of Hide and Seek plus Kick the Can.

One day I was exploring inside a burnt out church. I was only wearing sneakers. Then I stepped on a large spike, sticking out of a piece of burnt wood. When I put my weight down on the spike it went right through my shoe and foot and stuck out the other side. I was stuck to the board and couldn't get it off! There was a little black boy playmate with me who managed to pull the board off and help me limp the couple of blocks to my home. I never saw that little black boy ever again.

CHAPTER SIX

ADVENTURES OF PARK AND JOE

1948 - 1951

Park Joe

How We Met

I was a good swimmer and I spent a lot of time at the lake. A near tragedy occurred one day. My brother was trying to follow me in everything I did. I dove off the diving board into deep water and he jumped right in after me. He panicked because he could not swim in deep water. He had a strong hold on me and I couldn't swim or get him off my back. We were both drowning. A neighborhood kid named Park, swimming nearby saw our plight, grabbed us and pulled us into shallow water and saved us. This near tragedy began a saga, The Adventures of Park and Joe, as we grew up together as friends.

Later, we were all playing either in the water or on the dock. In his fun play, Park pushed me off the dock and into the water. I cut my foot badly on an underwater, wooden post in the bottom of the lake when I landed. The Life Guard gave me first aid. Then when my buddies saw what happened, they thought that Park had hurt me on purpose and they wanted to get Park and beat him up. He had sense to know what happened and he out ran them, even while running over gravel stones in his bare feet. Park impressed me and I hoped I would see him again.

Some weeks later after that incident, Park and I met in the woods where we were both hunting. We stopped to chat for a while. Park showed me a rabbit he had shot. And he offered me a chance to join him in cooking and eating it. I said I would build a fire. The wood chips that I used to make the fire came from a telephone pole that had been cut down recently. The chips were coated with black creosote tar. While the fire was burning it made a lot of black smoke from the creosote and it was clinging to the rabbit being cooked. We could not eat it that way so, in shame, I made another fire and felt like the tenderfoot I was. We finished cooking and eating the rabbit. After that we got better acquainted telling each other about ourselves.

Park was experienced and skillful at things done out of doors and in nature; skills in hiking, camping, hunting and the use of weapons for hunting. He was stocky built, had light brown hair and he was strong. He could walk so silently to stalk a deer the deer never heard him! He learned to hunt and fish because he was always hungry at home. Also, because of the environment he grew up in, he could get by on very little. He generally was not overly concerned with his personal appearance and cleanliness. The way he looked was fine with him.

I was skilled at fire building, camping and wood-lore. I was very active in Boy Scouts and new a lot about knot tying and building shelters from wilderness materials. I was tall and skinny with a big mop of black hair and a smile that was all teeth. I had big and long feet. Though I had a bad heart murmur, I still did most everything that Park could do. I was not very strong, but I was very tenacious. My personal hygiene was very good and I was most always clean and neat in my appearance.

Park's home, social and living environments were completely unlike mine or my family and my other friends. Park's father, Park Sr. worked as a laborer-carpenter for a local Antique Dealer. He was a tall, lanky, quiet man. His wife, Bertha was medium height and very obese. No offence, but her buttocks were as wide as a doorway. She also was a housewife and had diabetes. She was of Indian ancestry of which she was very proud and boasted about it to everyone. She was mean at times and treated Park badly. My Father worked as a Nurses Aide at the Canandaigua VA Hospital. My mother was a house wife with three children, a daughter, and two sons. My Grandmother, who was in her sixties, lived with us too. My being sickly a lot with a bad heart murmur, I tended, at times, to be a "Mama's Boy". In general I used proper manners the way I was taught in my home.

In Park's house in those days there was no electricity, indoor plumbing, or running water. They were just "poor white folks". My home had running water and indoor toilets. I always accepted and enjoyed Park's parent's friendship and hospitality. They treated me with admiration and pride, claiming me as another one of their sons. Park had three sisters. One was Annabelle, another was Clara. The one I liked best was Lena.

Why did Park and I bond so tightly? Why did I find him so magnetically attractive to me? Well first, Park was a true and loyal friend in every sense of the word. Secondly, he was not vulgar and rarely swore or spoke dirty talk. Third, he lived a carefree "Indian Like" life style which has always fascinated me. Fourth, I needed a change in my life, to get away from bad influences. I needed a true friend who was not a person that looked for and got into trouble or was lawless. I needed to have someone to take me away from hanging out with the local gang and its mischief. Park was the answer. So, that is the background of our friendship and the start of what I call "The Adventures of Park and Joe"!

Our Adventures

One of the first camps that Park and I made was in late August. We made camp just outside of Canandaigua city limits off of Rte 5 & 20 on and with the permission of Mr. Purple, the land owner. We camped under the tall pine trees in the hedgerow. Today this property is part of what is now Finger Lakes Community College. We each had blankets to sleep in and we slept side by side on either side of the fire. This was my first time camping out in the wilderness. We were cold that night. Each of us was quietly trying to tough it out without letting the other know that they were freezing. Our individual blankets were not enough to keep us warm. Finally out of desperation we decided to combine our blankets and sleep together for warmth. We kept a fire going for heat and light, but it was too cold to get in and out of the blankets to tend the fire. When we awoke, just before sun up, we became aware of some kind of activity coming from the top of the hill in front of us. Park said that he got up earlier and watched several deer moving by us headed for that hill top. After it got light enough to see we could make out a small herd of deer gathering at the top of the hill. We watched as pairs of deer charged one another in mating fights. It was my first observation of deer doing anything. I was so excited that my heart was racing wildly. I really liked to live adventures like this.

I had a 30/30 Marlin Lever-action rifle with an octagon barrel and Park had a 32 special Winchester lever-action rifle. We were hunting woodchucks. Park saw one, raised his rifle, aimed and fired. I was standing broadside of him. I stared in disbelief as I watched the useless lead slug of the bullet slowly roll out of the end of the gun barrel and drop silently to the ground! Park told me that he was using old bullets that his father got from the antique shop and gave to him. The powder was old. That was why the bullet did what it did!

Park was really effective as a deer hunter with a gun or bow. One day I saw him kill a deer with just his hunting knife. I will never forget that time. We came upon a wounded deer. It had been shot in one leg. The deer was dragging it and suffering badly. We felt we should put it out of it's misery. Park said that he wasn't wasting a bullet, but he would dispatch it with his knife. His knife looked like a broad, double-edged Roman short sword. He chased the deer for about 100 yards. His angle of approach brought him running along side of the deer. From there he brought the deer down with just one jab of his knife. Then he showed me how to skin and field dress it. When he had some meat cut up, we fastened some on sharpened sticks like a shish kabob. We made a fire and cooked a couple choice steaks. That was my first venison meal and it was great! Also, Park gave me and one of my friends some of his mother's stew one day for supper. It was made with woodchuck! I loved it but our friend did not.

One beautiful fall day we camped at the edge of the apple orchard on the Island Fruit Farm beside the outlet from Canandaigua Lake. Even though dark clouds predicted possible snow we didn't feel that it would happen. It was such a nice night so we didn't use our tent. Instead we just slept in our sleeping bags in the open beside the campfire. Next morning I woke up first. I had been very comfortable and snug. It was so warm that I was actually sweating. I peeked out of my sleeping bag being careful not to let the warm heat get out or let the cold in. Park had been sleeping right beside me, but when I looked for him, all that I saw was a beautiful white blanket of snow. Where was Park? When he awoke he came out from under the snow. We both had gotten completely covered with the snow. That made us warm and snug in our sleeping bags. That's when we realized that the predicted snow had come in the night.

That Fall Park and I built a cabin on the banks of the Canandaigua Lake Outlet on the land of The Island Fruit Farm. We had cut down trees and were putting them one on top of the other. But because the logs were too heavy for us to lift we had to change our design. So, we came up with a lean-to style cabin. It was just big enough for the two of us to enjoy it comfortably. We gathered up swamp grass and piled it on top to make a roof. Park said he had a stove and some glass for a window at his house about two miles away. We made a plan for getting those things down to our cabin site. We got a flat bottom row boat from a friend and poled the boat up the outlet until we were where the stove and glass were. We used a child's wagon and hauled the stove to the shore, then loaded it on the boat and poled it to the cabin. We installed the glass in the front wall of the cabin and put the stove inside. Many times that fall and winter we camped there, comfortable and toasty warm.

One of the foods we enjoyed while there were frog legs. At night we would take a flashlight and a big club, pole the boat up to where a frog was croaking and kept it still with the beam of light and then clubbed it. The frog was then tossed to Park who quickly cut off the legs to save them for our meal and threw the rest away. At times pheasants would walk out of the swamp grass and stand in front of the cabin. Guess what we would have for supper that day? We did not disturb the deer until deer hunting season.

We had friends named Gordon and Peggy Hill. They had two kids a boy and a girl when we first me them. Park and I lived with them for a while. Their house had electricity but no indoor toilet or plumbing. There was an outhouse latrine. They had to haul their water from a spring that was about 200 yards down the road. This house was located on the bank of the Canandaigua Lake Outlet just past where a railroad bridge, 100 feet high, went over the outlet. The Hills taught me to play the card games, such as Canasta and Pinochle. We spent a lot of evenings playing cards. We became good friends with them. When their twin daughters were born they named them after me. One was named Joanna and the other one Joleena. I really felt honored!

One day Park, Gordon, and I went Pheasant hunting. I did not have a license or a shotgun. All I had with me was my short barrel 22 rifle. I was across the field from them. As they hunted toward me they scared up a hen pheasant that flew right over me. As they saw me aim they shouted to me, "You'll never be able to hit it with just a 22 rifle." As it flew over my head I fired one shot and the bird fell to the ground dead! Was it luck or skill? Naturally I took credit for skill. Later Park took a shot at a cock pheasant. He hit it and it dropped about 100 yards away. At the same time another hunter across the field had shot a bird also, but his bird dog couldn't find it right away. He claimed the bird that Park had shot was his. He told his dog to bring the bird to him. He threatened us with his shotgun and ordered us to give it to him. No bird was worth getting shot. We gave it to him, but under protest.

Park bought a black stallion horse that year. His friend, Gordie Hill let him build a stable and stall in back of the house and allowed him to keep it on his property. One day Park borrowed a horse from a friend for me to ride. I had never ridden a real horse before. My riding experience had been gained on a merry-go-round horse. At first we rode mostly at a walk to let me get broken in, but after a while, when riding along the shoulder of the road, Park got bored and was ready for excitement! He decided to ride the horse across a newly plowed field at a full gallop as a shortcut to get back home quicker. He had ridden before and was good at it. Suddenly my horse decided to follow his, also running at a gallop. I'm sure I didn't look like any horseman anyone has ever seen, but I did stay on. It sure was fun but I wouldn't want to do it again.

Park's horse, a stallion, was extremely stubborn and hard to control. One

day when we were woodchuck hunting, Park on his horse, me on foot, Park was trying to sight-in his rifle at a woodchuck to make a shot and the horse would not stand still. Park got so angry at the horse that he swung the barrel of the riffle and hit the neck of the horse so hard that the barrel looked bent. He was happy when he sold that horse shortly thereafter!

In 1950 Park was 17 and about 5'6" and I was 16 and about 6'1". We had many common interests, and we bonded right away. It was also obvious to both of us that we were very much opposites. We decided to ignore all that and to become "Blood Brothers". So to seal it, we did what was the popularly accepted procedure. We gave ourselves a small cut to get blood on a finger. Then we rubbed our bloody fingers together to "mix" our bloods. In this ceremony we officially considered ourselves blood brother. We started a motto to describe our bond and brotherhood. It was "We're side by side…alone by each!" This means we were always side by side…yet we agreed to be ourselves and keep our different individuality, respecting the others' self. No one else knew what it meant, but we knew and remembered it as "Blood Brotherhood!"

Friendship with Park was not always happy. Once, while playing with our knives I got a bad cut across my finger and it bled a lot. Park's 'medicine' that he wanted to do, was to heat up a knife to cauterize the wound and stop the bleeding. But he couldn't do it, because he couldn't get me to stop running!

A farm incident with Park happened as we were putting the tractor away into the barn. I was backing up from the tractor that Park was driving. I was guiding him to get it into the barn. I tripped over a farm implement and as I fell I reached down to regain my balance and I stuck my arm and wrist into it and broke my wrist. My first broken bone! It felt like lightning hit me! I spent several weeks wearing a cast on my right wrist. I was able to go hunting even with one arm in a cast. I was able to wiggle my finger out from under the cast to shoot my shotgun.

Another time while working on a farm one summer using razor sharp, forked knives to cut and harvest the asparagus, we were taking a lunch break and playing Mumblie-Peg with our knives. Foolishly, I was reaching for my knife at the same time that Park was throwing his knife down. It struck my hand and opened quite a cut. The bleeding was profuse. The boss, though not happy about it, took me to a doctor. For our recklessness we got fired!

Next, we got a job planting trees for the Conservation Department. We would meet the boss and crew on the land where we were to plant trees. We each had a Mattock planting tool to plant evergreen trees that were about three to four inches tall. Park and I would race each other down the row while planting trees. The two of us could plant more trees in an afternoon, than what all the rest of the crew could do. That job brought us into some very beautiful countryside of the Bristol Hills. It was great working in the out of doors. All those jobs were labor type work. I began to wish I had stayed in school.

There was real excitement at Mr. Purple's land where there was an accumulation of years of straw production in a spot at the edge of his field. We found this pile of straw to be an ideal place to bed down when we camped. It was soft and warm. Eventually we built a hideout, concealed camp, on the inside of the straw pile. We used fallen tree branches to support the straw roof. Then one day as we were camped inside, Park, me, and my little white terrier dog named "Pal", were fixing breakfast using a very small fire. I pulled some straw down from the ceiling and put it on the fire to keep it going, but more straw than I wanted came down. Some fell on the fire and it blazed up and quickly caught the whole straw stack on fire. It seemed like Pal had springs on his feet as he went straight up through the ceiling and got out before any of us. We quickly charged through the wall of the straw pile for a fast exit to safety. Thick gray smoke rose up and it could easily be seen for maybe 10 miles. The sirens of the responding fire department were heard getting closer. We grabbed our gear and ran up the hill over a gully and into some thick woods to hide. Park had to drag me after him. I couldn't get my breath. After the fire died down we returned to the straw pile. The scene of the crime was all ashes. Mr. Purple was not angry, just concerned that we might have gotten burned in the fire. The straw pile he didn't consider to be of any value. This straw pile was located exactly where the main buildings of FLCC (community college) in Canandaigua are now. That was the last time Park and I camped on Purple's land. We had some great adventures there. We tested and developed our hiking endurance there by hiking as much as 10 miles every day.

Grandma Gates used to call us "Road Runners" and she nicknamed Park "Nighthawk". He was so proud of that that he designed and painted a figure of a Nighthawk on the trunk of his car. He also got a tattoo on his upper arm. He smoked. I didn't...except when his pack was almost empty. Then I would always want a smoke and end up smoking his last cigarette.

Not far from Canandaigua where we lived were the beautiful Bristol Hills. They have always reminded me of the Adirondack Mountains. On a camping trip in Bristol one time, in a place about where the Ski Center is located now, there was a nice brook that runs by there. We waded up that stream for about a mile to get away from the highway and we made a camp. The old man who owned the land said he wouldn't let us camp on his land, but we did anyway. We made a hidden camp, wading up the brook to a campsite so no one would ever see it. We shot woodchucks using our rifles. For supper there were some fish in the brook and we made fishhooks from safety pins and caught one or two! When we were ready to come home our pre-arranged ride did not show up, so we loaded our gear on our backs and started walking. We were in good shape from all the hiking we had done that summer. We walked all the way to the 5 & 20 highway at Toomey's Corners, over five miles away. We were exhausted then, so we called a friend to come and take us the rest of the way home.

We were growing to manhood together. On the way, we carried off one last kids stuff thing. Park's mother always had some rummage sale clothes around. We got some of them and dressed up...suits, shirt, tie, overcoats, and even hats. We looked like a couple of mobsters. Then we went to Geneva on the bus. We didn't want anyone in Canandaigua that we knew to see us. One of the places we went to that day was a bar. I had never drunk before. Park ordered liquor for me and I got drunk. In those days, there was a Sampson Air Force Base. The Air Force uniforms looked in color like bus drivers uniforms. We had to go home by bus, but intoxicated people were not allowed on the bus. I was trying to act sober and tried to be helpful to a person who I thought was an Airman. I told him "You can't ride the bus if you are drunk, so don't let the bus driver see you if you are!" It turned out that I was talking to the bus driver!

Because I was under the drinking age and in bad shape, with Park helping me, the bus driver let me ride on the bus home to Canandaigua.

I met a very nice family, Park's sister Lena, married to Walter Reish. They lived in a big house just outside of Canandaigua. They had two boys, Glen and Anthony and one girl, Ellen had a childhood crush on me. One Thanksgiving Day Park and I went deer hunting in their back woods. Afterwards we ate a big Turkey meal. Then Park and I polished off a quart of wine each. Park was fine. I got staggering drunk. I had my little white dog "Pal" with me and Lena had a big, big, German Shepard dog. Kidding, Lena told her dog to sic me and to take a bite out of me. My little dog jumped to my defense and surprised that dog. One bite would have finished him. Later I found some pictures of Park and I drinking that day. Boy was I smashed! Lena and Walt became good friends.

A few days later we went up to Saranac Lake to find a girl who had written me and sent her picture. It turned out the girl in the picture was her sister not her. The right girl was not as attractive. My cousin put them up to sending the letter and picture to me. In Saranac Lake we stayed at my Aunt Della's house at 46 Shepard Avenue and we decided to find a job and stay in town. We answered an ad that wanted people who could climb trees for lumber jack work. It was winter and icy. The trees were about 100 feet high. No way was I going to take that job! Park agreed.

While we were in Saranac Lake Park got bored from my talks about the view from the tip of Baker Mountain, located just outside of town. Park got the urge to climb it and see for himself. Remember, this was winter. I said that I would go with him. He decided that he wanted to make his own trail up instead of using the well worn trail that the local people used. Park made a trail as he went. He was a natural in the woods and all went well until we got to the top. Park got across the rocks quickly and safely. I was hesitant. The ice on the rock beneath my feet began slowly moving. Then Park took off his belt and handed it to me. With this assistance I made it across to the top. The view was fabulous! We could see for miles. The snow sparkled off the winter's landscape. It was a true winter wonderland. When we were ready to come back down I convinced Park to use the trail used by the local people. Thank God!

That summer we spent a lot of time roller skating at the Lakeside Roller Skating Rink on Keuka Lake across from Bluff Point, just about three or four miles beyond Branchport on route 54A south towards Hammondsport. We got to be good enough that we could do the pairs skates and it was a good way to meet girls. One girl we met there invited me to come to her hometown of Wilkesboro, Pa. to skate there. Park borrowed a van from his neighbor, supposedly to go skating at Lakeside, but instead we planned to go to Wilkesboro to meet the girl from roller-skating. I didn't have a driver's license, he did. After a long drive through NY and into PA we arrived at the right town and the right skating rink. But, what we didn't know was that it was closed on one night of the week only... Wednesdays. Guess what day it was? You guessed it. We didn't have much money, only enough for gas going home. We ate candy bars. On the route back home to Canandaigua we climbed the mountain road along the Susquehanna River. We stopped in a state rest area along the road. We were tired and broke and decided to camp out there because it looked as if it might rain. We had spread our sleeping bags out under a park bench and we were just about asleep when the PA State Trooper pulled up alongside of us. His appearing scared me out of my wits. He ordered us to vacate the rest area immediately! It was against the law to be camping there. He could have arrested us and given us a ticket. He was good about it and instead of doing that he told us to get in our car and take the road back home. We proceeded to do that until he was gone, then we got back in our bags and finished our sleep. At that time it was 4 o'clock in the morning. Luckily for us he didn't come back because we stayed there and camped all night.

Instead of driving back home to Canandaigua, Park drove us up through Pultney and into Prattsburg to rest at his cousins Harry and Genevieve (Jenny) Trenchard's house. Their hospitality was great. The time we spent overnight and half a day socializing made us so much more overdue bringing Park's friend's van back to him in

Canandaigua. Because we were so late returning the van without being advised why, the friend had an "All Points" search out for us. A State Trooper stopped us and warned us to get the van back immediately. The friend forgave us and was not angry at us.

About this time I was almost 17 and pretty well grownup. Park and I had been good friends for almost four years. He was now 18 years old and eligible for the draft for military service. Park went into the Army. He was stationed in Washington DC as part of the Honor Guard. When he was in the Honor Guard he was always spit and polished, clean and neat. I had gone to go to Saranac Lake in 1951 to earn my High School Diploma. That was not the end of our adventures though. We still had a few left in us. Like one time when Park was on leave and I was on Christmas vacation from school, Park offered to take me back to Saranac Lake. We were driving down route 3 at Cranberry Lake when a car came at us, slipping on the road and driving down our side of the road. He ran right into us! No one got hurt, but the van's fenders were so bent that the tires would not go around. My Brother and I had been sleeping in the back of the van. With the accident the hatchet that was hanging on the side of the van came down and the impact caused it to fall and land on my brother. It hit him but it didn't hurt him. He just got woke up. We were quite a distance away from Saranac Lake so Park improvised by taking his hatchet and cutting the fenders off the van so the wheels would turn. We had to drive back all the way to Saranac Lake with no fenders on the van. The insurance company paid for all repairs.

Park got out of the Army while I stayed in school in Saranac Lake. After that, Park got a girl pregnant and he was noble and married her. She gave him three sons. However, her sexual wanderings caused them to separate. She kept and raised the boys. We didn't see much of each other for quite awhile. Then he came to Castleton to drive the truck to help me move to Victor, N.Y.

About a year later, Park drove up to my house in Victor in a big, used Cadillac. He was excited about it and he wanted me to take a ride in it with him. He said that he might need my help. He drove to Lima, N.Y. Then he introduced me to Ellen and her husband, who was a timid and passive person. Then Park asked me to help him run away with Ellen, leaving the husband alone. It was obvious that the two of them had been planning it together and the only reason he wanted me along was as muscle, to help if the husband got violent. I did not agree with their action.

So, Park left with Ellen, and they ran away together to the Florida Everglades where Park had built a small shack for them to live in. There was no running water or electric. When the tide water came in it flooded the whole area around the shack. Alligators and big snakes swam in that area around the shack. Then they moved and relocated to Verona, Va. There Park built a small cabin out of pine logs, with a fire pit instead of a stove for cooking and heating. The cabin was built on the side of a mountain in a stand of Lodge-pole Pine trees.

One weekend, while I was working in Richmond Va., I drove my rental car the hundred miles to Verona to see if I could find them. The mailman said to keep going on the rural route until I saw his mailbox, so I did and found it. I waited there until Park came to get the mail. When he saw me he was elated and pleasantly surprised. He asked me to stay the night and I did. I woke up in the middle of the night with a big Blue-tick hound dog sleeping on my chest. I must have been using his bed! In the morning we talked while we ate breakfast and then had to say our good byes and I left to return to Richmond. The next I heard of them they had returned to Florida and settled in the center of the state in Morrison. They stayed there for several years and they prospered.

One weekend, when he was on vacation and visited me, we camped together at a place in Broomfield. We brought our guitars and our rifles. We played guitar and sang all the old songs. The ground where we were camped had a lot of phosphorous in the soil. It was an eerie sight to see pieces of sticks on the ground glowing in the dark of night. Ellen came out to find us so I could go to visit my father in the hospital, who had suffered a heart attack. That was the last time we camped together. After that Park developed serious heart problems. He fought a valiant fight for life; then he died peacefully in Florida.

Remembering Park

His spirit was free,
And it motivated me!
Over many years…as friends,
Sadly now our adventure ends!
With Park's wit and our brotherhood stilled,
The woods and trails where we walked are chilled.
But what my life hereafter might be,
Surely brotherhood again, for Park and Me!
(Side by side…Alone by each)

CHAPTER SEVEN

BACK TO SARANAC LAKE

Getting High School Diploma

1951 - 1952

Joe, Saranac Lake 1951

It was the year 1951, that my cousin Antoinette Willette was graduating from high school in Saranac Lake. I went up to Saranac Lake to be a part of the celebration. While I was watching the ceremony I was enthused by the idea of getting a diploma also. I mentioned that I would go back to high school and graduate with a diploma if I could go to school in Saranac Lake. My cousins got enthused with the idea and convinced my Aunt Della to let me move in with them and go to school there. My parents agreed to pay my Aunt rent for my room and board, so I moved up there from Canandaigua and registered for attendance in Saranac Lake High School in the class of 1952. I got settled into my Aunt Della's home.

Aunt Della

In 1951 she and her family were living at 46 Shepard Avenue in Saranac Lake. With the permission of my parents, she allowed me to come and live with her family so I could go to school. She also agreed to be my guardian while I attended school. I was admired, respected and loved by all my many cousins and relatives, who welcomed me and helped me feel at home. In that house, visitors were always welcome and afforded the finest Adirondack Mountain hospitality.

Although no one could ever replace my real mother, that year Aunt Della was like a second mother for me. At home I was over-protected, immature, and only semi responsible. My Aunt had house rules and requirements she expected me to abide by. She treated me as an adult and I appreciated the maturity she helped me to develop. She expected me to be mature enough to look after my personal needs and behavior. I also was expected to blend into her family's life activities and life style. She was the boss in her house and could be tough but loving. She always was proud of my achievements.

My Uncle Phillip was handicapped and confined to home. He was to be always given the utmost consideration and respect. At the time I lived there, my Aunt Margaret and my Grandmother lived there too. My Aunt's oldest daughter, Marceline Fanning, lived in part of the house, with her children. Aunt Della had a large family, most all of whom were grown and married and living in their own homes. There were only five children living there when I was there. I was to become part of the family.

My Aunt and the family were grand examples of Adirondack Mountain friendship and hospitality. Guests and visitors to her home were always made welcome and allowed to feel at home. She always showed a great deal of enthusiasm and had a smile in her voice. One habit she had (like other big busted women of her generation) was to stash her money in her bra. She called it "putting the money in the bank."

I really appreciated being allowed to be part of that family, to return to High School, graduate and complete my education. I'll always remember the nostalgic, homey atmosphere of Saranac Lake. The experiences I had there helped me mature into a person of whom I was proud. Saranac Lake has always felt like my home!

Cousin Marceline

Thanks to my cousin Marceline, the year I lived at 46 Shepard Avenue was made smoother, memorable and productive. Marceline became my mentor, as well as a friend. She and her four children lived in one part of the house, which was quite large. It had been a house that had been used as a curing cottage for TB patients. It had three stories plus a cellar, ten rooms, two baths, and four large screened porches. She was about in her forties at the time. She taught me to be a gentleman, and how to treat the ladies properly. She was a very good dancer and taught me well.

Marceline was easy to talk with. She had so much logic and common sense advice, or constructive criticism and she shared a wealth of experience on how to get along in the world. She didn't hesitate to disagree with me or tell me when I was wrong. Marceline always treated me with respect and empathy and she always noticed all my accomplishments with interest and pride.

Yes, my cousin Marcelene acted as a mentor for me, taught me to dance and to use social graces, manners and skills in dealing with people. I will never forget her help. She treated me as her brother. She was very proud of me. She instilled in me a lot of confidence and a strong self esteem which were very useful skills.

Summertime

That summer of 1951, while waiting for my senior year of school to start, I worked as a golf caddie at the Saranac Inn Golf Club. All of the exercise of walking18 holes twice a day, plus the good fresh mountain air and sunshine, going to bed at sundown and rising before sun up, built up my physical and mental endurance. This strengthened my self confidence, self esteem and satisfaction with myself. I learned to use discipline and psychology to prepare me for meeting and coping with the challenges and changes in my new life. I was enthusiastically looking forward to starting back to school and living in Saranac Lake again.

In Saranac Lake there was a place where teenagers could socialize. Many times I would bring my guitar there and would sit with my friends and sing songs and play guitar. It was called The Teen Canteen. At the coming election of officers, I accepted the duties as their PR Chairman. I wrote a "Letter to the Editor" of the local paper, the Adirondack Daily Enterprise. In it I compared being a teen living in a city like Canandaigua to the opportunities for a teen living in Saranac Lake. I especially referred to what there was, or wasn't, for teens to do or to be occupied in at Saranac Lake. By this time I was very well known by my future classmates and school hadn't started yet. I took some ballroom dancing classes before starting the school year. That's where I met my first girlfriend, at dance lessons. She was a freshman and I was a senior. Her name was Mary Ann Clancy. She wore Wood hue perfume. It became my favorite.

At this time I met Scott Jones. We became friends and began the adventures recorded in the next chapter.

School Year

At the start of the school year I was nominated for class President, but I declined because I hadn't been with the class that long and I supported another senior who had been with the class for the three previous years. I served as his campaign manager. We had a very large senior class of over 100 students. We won the election. In 1939-

40 I had been classmates when I was in the first and second grade with some of them. It was interesting finding out what they were like after a twelve year separation.

Being ambitious, I joined every group and activity that I could, such as Chorus, Senior Play and Fire Squad. I didn't when I was in Canandaigua because I believed that they filled openings by popularity or politics and I had to fit in to belong. In Saranac Lake I was happy most of the time because I kept myself very busy. I was pleased and proud of the things that I was accomplishing. The skills that I learned and used helped me to gain a popularity and recognition which was good for my ego and self confidence, but I also learned the value of humility and keeping myself from being conceited. Without a doubt I was not the same person who left Canandaigua.

In December of 1951 I played the lead male part in our Senior Play called Tish. I was Sheriff Lem Pike, with a handlebar mustache and rifle, and "romantic tendencies" as was reported in an article in the school paper, The Red and White, on November 3, 1951. The play was presented to a capacity crowd and reported by the local paper, the Adirondack Daily Enterprise, on Dec 8,1951.

Our nearest competitive school was Tupper Lake High School. It was about 25 miles from Saranac Lake. In chapter eight I have written how Scott and I met and became the best of friends. During the year after school I worked in the Grand Union grocery store as a clerk. This was my first Retail Store work experience. I liked it very much. Retailing became my second career. Sales work has always been the career of which I had the most experience.

Thinking back, I can remember the beautiful view from the windows of Saranac's School Library. There were three mountains shown in the background of the town with Lake Flowers sparkling like a blue jewel, prominent in the foreground. I did a watercolor painting of that scene in 1954 from memory and sent it to Mr. Harold Young, my favorite teacher, as a gift. I painted it during the time I was recovering from Rheumatic Fever in 1953-1954. There was always a wonderfully nostalgic aroma of the wood burning as a fuel used to heat homes. It made me feel peaceful and home-like. Our Alma

Mater expresses that nostalgia and our feelings of love for the mountain environment:

Saranac Lake Alma Mater
Circled round by mighty mountains,
Breathed upon by healing balsam,
Mirrored in the flowing river,
Blessed by Nature's soothing calm,
Stands our dear old Alma Mater,
Crowned with honor, crowned with love,
Crowned by all her subjects loyal,
True to her, all else above.
(Unknown)

There was to be a coronation ceremony to crown the King and Queen of the Teen Canteen on April 19, 1952 for it's seventh anniversary. I volunteered to take charge of decorating the Town Hall where the event was to be held. A medieval knight's round table was my theme. I made eight poster board shields with unique coat of arms designs, painted on them with appropriate colors, and hung them from the walls around the room to create a medieval atmosphere. Just before the Coronation/Variety show, I skipped school and took a Greyhound bus ride to Syracuse to go to see my parents for Christmas. I was trying hard not to be seen, because I was skipping school and starting vacation a day early. When I got on the bus for Syracuse, there were two female classmates already on the bus who were also skipping school. When word of it got around school, this trip was talked about all over school…me taking two girls on an out of town bus trip! Saranac Lake was a small town, remember? I had left the finishing of decorations for the event to committee members to do while I was gone. When I returned from vacation the decorations were finished and looked good. I was asked to be the Emcee of the event. There was one joke I told that got me publicity: It goes, Governor Al Smith was making a dedication of some sort, at Dannemora Prison. He thought carefully about how to address the prisoners and started his talk with "My fellow prisoners…" Then he thought again. He couldn't say that. So he started again, "My fellow citizens…" Oh no, then he remembered prisoners lose their citizenship when they go to prison. So he couldn't say that. He finally tried one last time and he said, "I'm so glad to see all of you here tonight!" This started the variety show off successfully with heavy laughter.

A newspaper article about the joke I told and the show was repeated by Eddie Vogt, columnist for the Adirondack Daily Enterprise, 2/11/52, telling that there were over five hundred people in attendance. Later, a second Variety Show was held in the Pontiac Theatre by popular demand. I emceed that one also. My success in my school speech work motivated my teacher, Mr. Young, to choose me to be the Emcee for the School's Annual Spring Festival Celebration, held in June, after graduation, on the front lawn of the school. This yearly festival was the most popular event of spring in Saranac Lake.

Doing well, I graduated from Saranac Lake in 1952. I majored in Industrial arts, earning an 85% overall average. I earned a school letter "S" for my sweater for work as a School Crossing Guard. With my camera I took most of the superlative candid pictures for our yearbook, Canaras, which is Saranac spelled backwards. I completed 20 hours of fire fighting fundamentals, and was member of the school's fire squad.

Saranac Lake is my native town and it always will be in my blood. I have and will always have a special attachment and love for that town, and it's people. I give my Willette relatives, Antoinette and especially my Aunt Della and cousin Marcelene Fanning great big THANKS for making this opportunity possible for me. Thanks also to my Mom and Dad for their support love and cooperation.

CHAPTER EIGHT

ADVENTURES OF SCOTT AND JOE

1951 - 1952

I was fated to meet John Scott Jones. I always call him Scott. When we met in the summer of 1951 I was waiting to become a senior in Saranac Lake High School and Scott was a student at Tupper Lake High School. I don't know what grade. He was younger than I. That summer, while waiting for school to start, I was attending the Teen Canteen, an entertainment center provided by the town as a place for teens to gather and stay off the streets and out of trouble. I was playing my guitar there and singing with my friends when I met Scott. Our towns were big rivals. Scott complimented me on my guitar playing and singing and offered me a job as a musician in his band. I was the new kid in town and anxious to meet and get acquainted with people. Looking back, I see now how naive and gullible I was. He conned me into walking 20 miles, carrying my guitar and suitcase, to get to the place where his band was. There were a couple of other guys with Scott who I thought were other band members too. Well, yes it was 20 miles and we made it to where he was taking me. It turned out to be the Saranac Inn Golf Course and specifically the caddy house where they all worked as caddies. No one was a musician or had a band. Well, Tupper Lake scored again!...at my expense! I was a good sport about it and we all became friends. Scott became my best friend and has remained so to this date, after 53 years. He must have felt a bit guilty for conning me, because he talked the Caddy Master in to hiring me to start the next morning. I had never done anything like golf or known anything about Golf Caddying. The Caddy Master had a routine for getting us up each morning; he had an ax handle and hit our beds to wake us up. If we didn't have a mattress on top of us in the morning we would get hit with the ax handle and it hurt. I learned quickly to put that mattress on top of me before going to bed. This was only the first of such episodes in our friendship.

We bonded with each other from then on. Scott was from a family of mountain people the same as I was. We share the lure of the Adirondack Mountains and their people. We also share the same religion and philosophy of life. We are both accepted as a member of each other's family. I greatly admired his mother and father. His Grandfather was a real independent mountain man. Scott has two sisters, Saundra and Janice. Scott Jones has always reminded me of Randolph Scott, the movie actor, because of his square cut jaw, his strong build, and his air of strength, coolness and confidence. Yes, Scott has many times reminded me of that actor.

Through Scott, I became known and met friends from Tupper Lake such as "Boogo" LePorte, and his sister Beulah, a cute, dark haired, French, Catholic girl. Now, Boogo played an end position on Tupper's Football team, Saranac's biggest rival team. I knew that Boogo was very much smitten with the girls on our cheerleading team. What an opportunity this was for me to get my "licks" in as retribution for the con-job they did on me in the summer, to caddy at the Saranac Inn. Some of these football team members were the ones who were in on that con. My plan was to ask our cheerleaders to yell Boogo's name when the play came around past him on their end of the field. They did and he turned his attention to them when he heard his named being called, as the ball was passed to him. The result of that botched up play was that Tupper missed making a touchdown that may just have been what caused them to lose the game that day! Sorry folks, but we did things like that. (We were friends!) And that reminds me of another incident related to them, us and football.

One September Friday afternoon after a football game in Saranac Lake, we were all walking down to Meyer's Drug Store to get cokes and celebrate Tupper's win over Saranac that day. In Saranac we had to walk down a steep sidewalk and then pass over a bridge at the end of the lake. On the way downtown I was mouthing off and ribbing them that they were winners only by the sheerest luck. I guess I over did it. Suddenly, they picked me up to throw me in to the lake. Remember, this was in September in the mountains. However, I don't remember being wet and cold, so must be it was only a threat. Was it something I said?? Friends do those things. Right??

One afternoon, Beulah invited me to have supper with her family. I think they wanted to size me up before Beulah went on a date with me to a school dance. All her family teased her, "Was this going to be a date?" She had an older brother, who was a lumberjack. I felt his arm muscles and they were as hard as iron. I made it a point to become friends with him. He split a couple of cords of wood before supper. I gladly helped him stack the wood. I don't know when I had so much fun! I guess I must have passed the test, because we went to the dance with her family's blessing. That night at the dance, everyone was friendly and they taught me how to Square Dance. Beulah was a very good dancer. We had a good time, but she was too young for me.

Another thing that happened one winter day in Saranac, I didn't have skates so I just watched the people skate, wishing I could too. In the skating shack, where the skaters went to keep warm, there was a pair of skates hanging on the wall. They were unclaimed and just my size. The caretaker said I could keep them. I did. Scott and I joined the other skaters. We decided to try to get dates for that night. I was asking a girl named Carol to go out with me. She shocked me by asking if she could date Scott and we would double-date, since I knew a lot of girls in Saranac who would go out with me. So that's what we did! Nice buddy, right?

This was the scariest ride I ever had. We hitch-hiked a ride from Tupper back to Saranac in the winter. There was not a lot of snow on the road, but it was slippery. The driver was a speed freak. He drove at speeds up to 100 miles per hour. I was petrified! Was I ever happy to be alive in Saranac at the end of that ride!

At a later time and place, in Phelps, NY, we went to a local hangout bar looking for girls. Scott and I sat in the car in the parking lot instead of going inside. We discussed life, girls, sex, and philosophy. We got to know more about each other. We expressed our deepest feelings, moral codes, and techniques for dealing with women. We also shared our thoughts about religion, friendship, drinking and our families. After the talks we realized that we had built a lasting bond with each other. We became like brothers. The bond has lasted for over 53 years! Scott has always shown up when Judy and I have faced hard times, like sickness, death, etc. An example was when I was in the Plattsburgh hospital waiting to go to Vermont for Open Heart Surgery. Scott managed to bring my kids in to me so I could say good by to them; should the worst happen.

How is this scenario!...One night wanting to go to a basketball game at Tupper's high school in 1951, Scott told me he would sneak me into the game. First, he smuggled me into the locker room by pulling me in through a window, then I kept cool and kept walking to the bleachers and I sat down to watch the game. I imagine that people wondered "who is that guy?" It was an exciting thing to do. Just another Scott and Joe adventure!

Most of the times in my adventures in Tupper Lake the people treated me with abundant friendship and respect. But one night in the Wakeshia bar, where Scott and I were double dating and enjoying the dancing, the girl that Scott got me a date with was the girlfriend of the guy sitting next to me. He was looking and talking at me in a threatening way. The one thing Scott didn't tell me was that this girl was only 16 years old. I was 21. I could have gone to jail for that! He took out a knife and was swinging it around in a threatening way. I told him that if that knife was supposed to scare me that he ought to know that I grew up in the city where knife fights were common. I told him that I was not scared by the knife. He finally put the knife away and then said that I could dance with his girl anytime that I came to Tupper. He was friendly after that.

Scott and I had many other adventures over 53+ years, and we have remained best friends.

CHAPTER NINE

RHEUMATIC FEVER

College Years

1953 - 1954

Recovering from Rheumatic fever

Dad

In 1952 I came back to Canandaigua from Saranac Lake after I graduated from High School. I started working at a Star Super Market. I worked there about a year and a half. During that time I bought my first car, met a girlfriend from Naples and I would go back and forth from Canandaigua to Naples some times till three in the morning. Then I would park my car in the store parking lot, sleep in my car until my boss woke me up when it was time to go to work and I would start things all over again. Eventually my body got run down and I got Rheumatic fever. I had to be bed ridden for 8 months. I kept busy doing stuff, but could not get out of bed. I used the time to write songs and learn to play the guitar. I painted art work to keep busy. Somewhere around 1953 the doctor said I could get up and try to walk around some. I couldn't at first though, because of being bedridden so long. The first thing I had to do was to learn to walk again. I walked around home at first. Then one day my dad took me to town. He wanted to drive me home, but I wanted to walk back. My father didn't think that I could do it but I thought I could. He let me try to walk. I couldn't walk very fast or walk proper, but little by little, as I walked and then rested, I made it home. My self esteem drove me to continue to walk and work hard to get my strength back. After a few months I did get stronger. A couple of my girl friends took me out to Square Dance. They thought I could do it and I did! I couldn't really square dance but I enjoyed being there and being out with girlfriends. One friend in Wayland, NY was going to get married and he wanted me to be his best man. His name was Barney Johnson. The first time he took me to Wayland for the wedding was the first time that I was out in a year. Everything looked so green and wonderful. It was amazing! The wedding was fine, but the place where the reception was held was on the second floor and I couldn't go up the stairs. However, everyone knew I had been sick and treated me real good. I sat downstairs and listened to everything going on upstairs. When I needed a drink someone got it for me and they made me real comfortable.

When I was strong enough to get back to work, I wasn't able to go back to work in the grocery store. The manager knew Mr. Willis, a local store owner and he recommended me for a job. I first met "Mickey" (I called him Mr. Willis) in 1954. He was seeking a young man, with excellent references, to hire and train as his assistant, to manage his clothing store, Willis Men's Store in Canandaigua. The manager from the Star Super Market gave me a glowing reference about my character and honesty. Mickey offered me a job opportunity based on how impressed he was with me as a candidate. Part of the offer was the promise to teach me all phases of Retail Business Management. I accepted. Mickey was great to work for. He treated me very well and gave me his full trust. He was a very effective teacher. He was very patient, while he passed on to me his 30 odd years in the operation of a business.

One year he took me with him on a trip to Buffalo, N.Y. to order the next season's inventory. At that point I had never before stayed in a motel or hotel. We stayed overnight in one big city hotel, including meals. We both shared the same bed that night (can you imagine how nervous I was!) We had an opportunity to discuss our futures. He treated me as a son. On the drive home we discussed an offer that he sincerely hoped I would accept. He offered to sell the business to me on reasonable yearly payments . .and . . if he passed away, the debt would cease and the business would be mine.

This was a very generous offer, but there were two things that made me reject it. One was that I had already enrolled and registered to attend Geneseo State College. I would be the only one in my family to go to college. It was just two weeks away. Secondly, I did not feel I was mature enough to handle the responsibility of ownership of a business.

I did go to school at Geneseo, in January 1954, in the second semester of the school year. But the lack of sleep from a chiming church bell ringing every hour plus the stresses of college work wore me down physically, coming right after being bedridden eight months from Rheumatic Fever. I suffered a nervous breakdown. I was having trouble sleeping and remaining aware of my surroundings. My Father had to come to get me from college and bring me home to Canandaigua. I had worked so hard to get to go to college. I was the first in my family who had gone to college. I felt that I was a failure! I was again bedridden at home this time with depression.

While I was home from school I kept all my books and read them all. I studied all the subjects and wrote a term paper named "The Comparisons of Roman and Greek Architecture." I was still learning more about playing my guitar and also in writing songs and short stories. Then I signed up for post graduate course at Canandaigua High School. I finished that in 1955. After that I longed to go back to Geneseo to prove I didn't run and hide, defeated and ashamed.

After a few months rest and medical help, I was bored with things as they were. I decided that I wanted to go out dating girls again. My confidence and self esteem had returned and I was ready to face life again and be in the world. Mickey helped me cope with things and that helped me get back to normal.

Tony Pesco, from Canandaigua, a high school classmate, became one of my best friends. We were about 19 or 20. He was happy to join me on my trips to Geneseo because the girls were five to one there. We had lots of good friends there and so much fun. We had a pact that when we drove home late at night each would watch for the other's car that might be parked (while the driver slept). We would check to see that our friend was ok and wake him up. This happened many times and the pact worked well.

CHAPTER TEN

JUDY AND OUR FAMILY

1956 - 1957

Love Blooms

A Lovely Lady!

How We Met

Our first meeting was on September 26, 1956. It was fate, like a set of romantic, love-story events. It happened like this:

I was a bachelor in my twenties, living in Canandaigua. I often came over to Geneseo, to date college girls. Judy was attending Geneseo State College. She was in her freshman year. She was seventeen and a very pretty blue-eyed college girl.

One night, she was attending a dance at her college called a 'Gangster Party'. Both of us had come to the dance stag. The music was great and I felt like dancing, so I looked around the dance hall looking for a good dancing partner. I saw a girl across the dance floor that I wanted to dance with. I walked across to where she was, planning to ask her to dance. Just as I reached her, she joined another man and started dancing. Well, I hadn't planned on that. It left me standing alone and feeling very conspicuous. Quickly though, I thought of what action I should take next. Since Judy's back was to me and I had never met her, I felt that she would never know that I hadn't intentionally come over to ask her to dance.

She had beautiful blue eyes. We walked out onto the dance floor holding hands. I held her closely in a dance. As we danced, I realized how nice a figure she had…and I liked that! She was a good smooth dancer…and I liked that! She had beautiful blue eyes, holding me in her gaze and seeming to like what she saw…and I liked that! She spoke with a pleasant, cheerful, happy voice…and I liked that! She asked lots of questions about me that showed she was sincerely interested and cared about me…and I liked that! Then I realized that I had never asked her name and I didn't like that! So I quickly corrected the situation. When I heard that her name was Judy Swartzenberg, and I told her that my name was Joe Beauchemin, we both laughed over the facts that we each had similar problem names…easy first names and long, ten letters, hard to pronounce last names. This gave us a bond to start. We danced happily and only with each other the rest of the dance…and we liked that! Some called it "Love at first sight", and we liked that!

Courtship

Our courtship was a little frantic with her in college at Geneseo and me living in Canandaigua. In addition, her father insisted that Judy complete the school year she was in. We both agreed to have some separation time so that Judy could study and successfully complete the year. It was agreed that we would only see each other on weekends until the school year ended, then her parents would give us their blessing for us to become engaged. Asking her father was an ordeal, but being a fair and wise person (and plenty scared at times); we discussed engagement, with acceptable terms and a satisfactory outcome.

We didn't make it, separating till the end of the school year, but we really tried. I had to hold on to the diamond for months until I could give it to her! We became engaged on January 27th 1957. She was almost 18 and I was nearly 23. As the days went by, we both felt that God had answered our prayers. That He had chosen for us and sent us someone to love and to share our lives with. We each had always had longed for that.

We planned our wedding for September 7, 1957, however I almost made Judy a widow instead. The causes were two serious auto accidents that I had prior to our wedding. The first occurred just outside of Lima, NY. I was trying to pass a car on the right side as the other car was signaling to make a left turn. The driver suddenly changed his mind and swung back into the right lane and I hit his car from the rear. This resulted in over $300 damage to my car. Fortunately there was no injury to other people or myself. My speed and poor judgment were at fault.

The second accident was because I was trying to hold too many jobs prior to my wedding. The first was as a salesman for Raff's Hat Shop in Rochester, NY. The second job was as a salesman in the J. C. Penny's Store in Greece, NY. After work hours there, I caught a city bus and later a Greyhound bus, went the 10 miles to Canandaigua for work at Roseland Park as a counterman. This most serious auto accident happened in the morning at 8:30 on the way in to work. I ran into a city bus on Monroe Ave. in Rochester, NY. A man stopped to offer his help. He said seriously, "What happened?" I said, "I don't know,…I Just got here." The steering column felt like it had imbedded itself in my chest. The steering wheel was bent downward, in the shape of a "U". A doctor came by and he quickly examined my chest and said that there were no ribs broken and to sit still until the ambulance arrived. Because of the way I was holding onto the steering wheel between my hand and thumb, my thumb was torn away from the main part of my hand. It was possible to look into the tear and see the nerves, which looked like white worms, UGH! From the impact, the key was imbedded in the flesh of my right leg. Strange thing though, my pant leg was not even torn or cut. But, the most dramatic wound was an abrasion on my forehead above my left eye. That was where my head hit the sun visor instead of the front window. It bled profusely all over my new suit and tie, and the front seat. The ambulance had been called. When it finally arrived they quickly did what they could to stop the bleeding. I was conscious but not coherent, or in pain. They took me to the Emergency Room at Strong Memorial Hospital. It was about a block away from the accident, but the ambulance took half an hour to get to me. They stitched me up and then put on a lot of gauze bandages. I called my brother and my father to come and bring me home so that my mother wouldn't see and get hysterical.

On the way home my brother stopped by the garage where the tow truck had towed my car. He could not believe that I had survived the wreck. There was blood all over the front seat and the motor had been pushed up into where the glove compartment was. I looked in the glove compartment and there was the motor. The worst was that I didn't have collision insurance on the car. So I had to make payments for two more years and not have the car to drive. I got my old car back from my father. He gave it to me to so I could get to and from work. The accident happened just two weeks before my wedding. I explained to everyone that the scar on my forehead was where Judy hit me with a rolling pin when I tried to change my mind about getting married.

We were married at St. Patrick's Church in Victor, NY on September 7, 1957. Tony Pesco sang at our wedding…"My Funny Valentine". He has a beautiful voice! We have been good friends for nearly 50 years.

CHAPTER ELEVEN

MARRIAGE & EARLY FAMILY

1957 - 1959

1957 - "A Great Pair!"

Judy's Family

Eunice Swartzenberg was Judy's mother. She was born on April 7, 1907. Eunice was the best Mother-in-Law a man could ever ask for. We could always count on her to help us if we were in need. I liked her style...not interfering unless we asked her too. Judy's father was Milton Swartzenberg. He was born on June 17, 1906. He owned a Hardware store in Victor NY. She has two sisters, Dorothy Dickinson (July 30, 1933) who is married to Les Dickinson (Jan. 19, 1929), and Rita Casey (Sept. 2, 1935) who is married to Larry Casey (Aug. 1, 1932) and one brother, James Swartzenberg (Dec. 8, 1941) who is married to Bonnie Swartzenberg (May 26, 1948).

I was still working as a sales clerk at Raff's Hat Store and got permission to take a week off to go on my honeymoon. We had planned to go on our honeymoon to Washington DC, but changed plans and went to Canada and New England. The following Monday was a Holiday and Monday was my normal day off so I didn't come back to work until Tuesday. As I entered the store, the boss told me not to take my coat off because, when I didn't come in to work on Monday he had hired his brother-in-law to take my place. I think he had always thought that with a name like "Bushman" I was Jewish, until I got married in a Catholic Church. Jewish people always take care of one of their faith first. That's the real reason that he gave his brother-in-law my job. I understood and was not surprised.

So there I was, married and with a wife to support and I had no job and no income! I was in shock. I was drinking coffee and reading the want ads and worried what to do all morning. Then I answered one ad that looked good. I walked four blocks to Hathaway Bakery because I didn't have a car anymore. I was hired as a home delivery door-to-door route salesman, at $20 more money per week than I was getting paid at Raff's Store. Judy worked at the Rochester Credit Bureau then. Our first apartment was on Park Ave. in Rochester.

We were blessed when on July 11, 1958, Judy gave us our first child. She was born in St. Mary's Hospital, in Rochester, NY. I remember my first sight of her at the hospital directly after she was delivered. She was all bloody and wrinkled and I was ready to give her back to the hospital to keep! But she cleaned up well and I was very proud of her and decided to keep her. She was a beautiful girl. We named her Josette (little Joe). We thought that was just the perfect name for our daughter. We named her after her Daddy and a French lady named Josette. On the way home from the hospital I stopped at Genesee Park beside the Genesee River. I said some prayers of thanksgiving that she was healthy and I was a father and Judy was alright. Joy of joy, I had become a Father!

She was a very good baby and she was very smart. Judy taught her how to crawl up the stairs and then come back down sitting and bumping her rump down safely, one step at a time. Josette learned that very well. That gave Judy more ease, knowing that Josette would not be climbing and falling down the stairs and getting injured.

I was real thankful for getting the Hathaway job income, but after a year I looked for more income doing part-time work. In 1958, I watched a Sarah Coventry sales representative (FSD) conduct a Jewelry Home Fashion Show at a friend's house. I saw her earn as much money in three hours doing clean, pleasant business work selling the jewelry, as I had to work after eight long hours for that same amount of money, bouncing in a truck. I joined Sarah Coventry on a part-time basis and I liked being an FSD, but when the Area Manager pressured me to take on full time management, I started doing badly and decided to quit the FSD job. This was my first failure in my career at Sarah Coventry.

For about a year we lived in Rochester, NY, but I didn't like living there. I was not happy and I had a strong longing to return to the Adirondack Mountains and Saranac Lake where I was born, had family, and had graduated from high school. Judy supported the desire to raise our family away from the city of Rochester. We made a decision (mostly because she wanted to see me happy.) She gave her support and we decided that I would immediately quit my job and move to Saranac Lake. We would live on faith. We were poised on the brink of disaster, but the three of us were ready for future adventures, or disaster!

The move to Saranac Lake had all the trappings and feelings of a pioneer family moving West in a covered wagon. I borrowed a truck from one cousin and got the physical help of another cousin, who was extremely obese, to be the driver of the truck. We packed everything we owned in the truck and tied a canvas over the top of everything. The truck's load area was only about 8' x 4' x 3' high. Within this space we had to pack all household, suitcases, baby needs, recreation, and sports equipment. This was all covered over and held on by the canvas with ropes tied on and more ropes wherever we had to. We hung pails, mops and an ironing board on the ropes. Yes, this resembled a covered wagon, and sounded like it at times.

There was only one seat in the truck and squeezed in this were the obese driver, Judy holding baby Josette and me holding on to a treasured lamp for dear life! Seated like this, we traveled the over 300 miles to get to our new home in Saranac Lake. I must mention that all the way Josette took it all in stride. Mama (Judy) had her hands full, and at times, her bladder as well. Papa (Joe) was a physical and nervous wreck, worrying about the lamp and his full bladder, plus a terrible craving for a cigarette. So, there we all were, hanging in there! It seemed like forever, but we finally made it. It was September, 1958, just in time to prepare to meet old man winter. Well, at least we got away from Rochester city living and now we were ready to live in the Adirondacks. All we have to do was find a place to live and then a job and survive.

After a short while I got a job with a newspaper and magazine distribution company in Saranac Lake, for just $50 a week for 40 hours of work and no raises expected. I wanted to be there in Saranac Lake badly enough and was willing to accept that low income. I thought I could make a go of it.

To my surprise my first job duties were to fill orders for magazines and books and to pack them between newspapers that had the customer's name printed across them. My supervisor was the father of one of my high school classmates. He was very meticulous and governed the time it took. When I became good at that phase of the business, I was assigned to learn the newspaper phase of the business. My cousin, Ray Willette, supervised me and taught me. I discovered that preparing newspapers was a high skill. The owner could insert fillers into Sunday papers and count them faster than the eye could follow. Putting inserts into the main part of the paper created a very rhythmic slapping sound that showed one's amount of experience and skill. I was also amazed at how quickly that he could count out the quantity of papers needed for a customer's order. He would separate four or eight papers at a draw and count by eights to reach the total quantity of papers to fill the customer's order. Then he would label the customer's bundle of papers and tie rope around it. Putting a ring-knife on his little finger he cut the rope. He could tie, bind, and finish a customer's order all in one motion. He was like poetry in action. I learned the skills to do the work but I never dreamed of ever getting that good.

On Saturdays we had to take a big box-truck and drive all night to Albany, NY to meet the train from New York City, carrying the Sunday papers for the Adirondacks and Saranac. On the way back, some of us would navigate and drive and the rest of us would ride in the back with the newspapers so we could count and bundle paper orders to be dropped off and delivered on the trip back to Saranac. It was exciting.

My weakness was that I was not a very assertive driver. I did not know how to "double-shift." Every mountain hill I drove up, I would have to coast back down and start up again. We had time constraints to consider for making our paper drops on time. So, I was not very satisfactory. I never was sent on any other trips, thankfully.

For a hobby I joined a Field Archery Club and attended weekly field archery shoots in surrounding towns. During the season I enjoyed hunting deer with my bow and arrows. My most embarrassing hunt, but also the funniest, was this one. Being as quiet as I could, I had stalked a group of three deer for over an hour and they had not been aware of me. They were feeding with heads down, about 25 feet away from where I was. There was some tall grass between me and where they were grazing. I had only four arrows with me. I knelt down and aimed my first arrow at one deer in the group and released the arrow carefully. The arrow came down between the deer's back legs and it didn't even flinch. So I strung another arrow and adjusted my aim and then released the second arrow. In flight it appeared that it was going to score a good hit, but it had just a little too much elevation and it breezed over the head of my target deer. All three deer kept on feeding in place with no concern for the arrows coming in on them. My third arrow, I was positive was going to be a hit so I snapped it off instinctively. It had too much elevation again and it missed. Well, not to worry, I still had my fourth arrow. I got in the best shooting position and concentrated on aiming to get a killing shot on one of those terrific deer. My heart was racing wildly in anticipation because this looked like it was the one. But fate, in the form of an unseen tree branch caused the arrow to be deflected and it too was a miss. I was so mad and frustrated that I came charging out of the grass swinging my bow at the deer and screaming all kinds of bad things at them and scared them out of the field.

Winter came in Saranac Lake and it was hard to make ends meet financially because of the added expense for heat. I needed to get more income and I was laid off from my job. I took a part time temporary job with Bill Meyers of the drug store chain, Meyers Drug Stores, at the store in Saranac Lake. I walked to work in 20 to 30 below zero weather. I was a clerk, working in the basement of the Saranac Lake Hotel cleaning up and salvaging drug store inventory stock that was brought there after a fire at their Elizabethtown store. I still needed a full time job. Bill told me that his brother, Norman, in the Plattsburgh store was looking for help. Bill suggested I call him about a job there. I did and was on my way over to Plattsburgh to be interviewed by him in the store when my car skidded off the snow and icy road and ended up in the ditch. A farmer saw the car go in the ditch and he came with his tractor to help pull me out. He easily pulled me out and he got me back on the road. I continued going to Plattsburgh. Thank God for the Adirondack Mountain code of helping your neighbor! I got a job as a sales clerk in the drug store. I also got an apartment rented in the Federal Housing Project in Plattsburgh, rent based on income. I was sure glad I got it. I gave notice to all those concerned and packed our possessions on a truck and we moved to Plattsburgh, to 25 Tyrell Avenue.

My Uncle Leo Gates towed me and my old car to the junk yard where I got $50 cash for it. Then my uncle took me to a car dealer in Plattsburgh that he did business with. He negotiated and got me a useable car for the same $50. He went back and asked for Green Stamps and got them too. He and my Aunt Elizabeth were God sends to Judy and me.

An exciting thing happened after I had been working for six months in Meyers Drug Store. One morning I was in the cellar stockroom of the drugstore, putting cigarette cartons on the shelf. There was a loud explosion noise and the ceiling seemed to rise up and then come back down and splattered dust all over me. I went to see what had happened. What I saw was that the furnace had exploded and thick, black smoke was rolling quickly toward me. I reacted quickly and went upstairs to the sales floor and got customers and employees out of the store to safety. The owners weren't in the store at the time so I drove to their house to notify them of the fire and bring them to the store. When I returned to town, the flames were licking up through the roof and walls of the store and a crowd of sight seers had gathered on the sidewalk across the street from the burning store. I just joined the crowd and stood there watching the fire. Rumors circulated that a man had been trapped in the store (me) and had died in the fire. They didn't know I had left to go get the owners. No one could find me, so they thought I got trapped and died in the fire. The local radio station WIRY was broadcasting this happening and said that it was me who died. Judy heard it and was petrified, until I contacted her and told her that I was alive…and well.

After the fire I didn't want to work for Norman Myers anymore. I didn't like his way of doing business especially at payroll time. A job at Gordon's, the drug store down the street came open. I went there and was hired. Later Norm bought out the Gordon's Store business (my luck), so I left to seek another job. By this time I had earned a good reputation in Plattsburgh, as a good retailer with excellence in customer service.

Within a week I accepted a position as Store Manager of M. A. Hardy's and Son, a plumbing and heating retail store. The owner was Lester Hardy. My mission was to take over management of their new home appliance department to replace the previous manager, who was costing them too much for his salary. In the first year I had tripled the sales and had a very satisfactory appliance business, but I was working for 'peanuts'. I liked the Hardy's and enjoyed the work. I felt my family was entitled to more benefits that more income would give us and I should move on.

Another opportunity came to me in 1959. The local Sarah Coventry Branch manager, whose husband was in the Air Force at Plattsburgh AFB, was being sent to another duty station. So the area manager was looking for a replacement to take over as Branch Manager. Word got around that I had worked in Sarah business before in Rochester. I was asked if I was interested in training for the job, and I said, "Yes!" I started my official "Sarah" career at the beginning level of a FSD (Fashion Show Director). The jobs were to book shows and demonstrate the Sarah Coventry Jewelry to build up sales volume and to build a unit of FSD's. Then achieve a unit sales volume to qualify for consideration as the replacement Branch Manager. In my first two weeks I had held 6 shows, with award winning sales volume and had 21 future bookings, plus I hired my first recruit. My part-time income was double that of my full-time job. I was doing an outstanding job and was receiving praise and awards for my performance.

Then a trauma struck! I had some teeth filled and a strep germ infection entered my blood stream, which developed into Sub-Acute Endocarditis, an infection on my heart valve. It caused me to be hospitalized for about six weeks while doctors tried to find an antibiotic that would kill the strep germ. This was life-threatening. I worried about my wife and children. What if I should die? Finally, a new antibiotic was found that attacked the infection and gradually I recovered. I had to spend the next few weeks at home resting and recovering. Meanwhile, my job at Hardy's was gone and the management opportunity with Sarah Coventry was postponed. We lived on a small disability income and faith.

On June 10, 1959, I was extremely happy and proud for Judy and I to have a son. We were especially thankful that he was healthy and did not have any heart problems. That was something that might have been genetic or inherited from me. We had planned to name our first son after my best friend, John Scott Jones. That name fit, because both Scott's were happy with that christening.

She's Always by My Side

Judy is her name, treat her with respect.
She'll brighten up your day,
With her bright smile and cheer in her voice,
She's my pride and is always by my side.
The day she became my bride,
She stood right there by my side.
And after fifty years of marriage,
She's still there by my side.
No man ever had a better partner for a wife!
She's loving, loyal and true.
As she travels with me through life,
She kept her promises like I asked her to.
I'm blessed, with her by my side.

Other words of praise for Judy!

All my love and respect I give in devotion to you Judy, as my wife. You have been a blessing from God to me. I have always been happy and contented with you. You have brought me love, romance and a family of whom I'm proud. You bring me strength during all my adversities. With your devotion and respect for me you inspire me to overcome them and lead me closer to God. Your pleasant and cherry voice has always brought me strength and enthusiasm for life.

Your loving husband, Joe, your Honey!

CHAPTER TWELVE

FAMILY AND CAREER CONTINUED

1960 - 1968

Scott was always an energetic, active, and smart child. He seemed to radiate an aura of maturity from an early age. He was very generous with his things. His mom could always depend on him to be helpful and considerate. He had cute dimples and a contagious smile. He liked to be my "right-hand man" and was very helpful when he would assist me to do things. But, he also could be very insistent on doing things his own way. For example, one night when we lived in Castleton, Scott would not stay in his crib and go to sleep. I told him that if he was going to stay up all night that he would have to do it with me. I stood against a wall and made him stand there beside me. He said that he wanted to go back to bed to sleep, but I said he couldn't now, until he was ready to stay in bed and not crawl out of his crib anymore. Finally he got tired and started to slouch down the wall and I would not let him slouch to the floor and sleep. After an effective time, I asked him where he was supposed to sleep. He said, "Crib." I told him to climb back into it and not to forget tonight and to stay in his bed from now on when his mom puts him there...or he will have to stay up all night with me! To my knowledge he never tried that stunt again.

After my recovery from Endocarditis I had returned to the job training as a Sarah Coventry Manager in Plattsburgh. I did an outstanding job of recruiting new FSD's and maintained satisfactory sales production. That fall, I was promoted to Branch Manager of Plattsburgh when Branch Manager, Jean Barnett left. My total branch sales in one week exceeded $10,000 and I had increased the file count of the branch by 35 new recruits. I made a paycheck that first week of over $1,000. But then, three weeks later my weekly paycheck was only twenty-five cents. Working direct sales on a commission basis was like that and just too variable for me at that time to still provide security for my family.

Judy's mother, Eunice really earned my respect early on in the way she coped with the death of her husband, Milton in 1960. After this, she kept their hardware store going by being the manager and running a one person operation. She was very much a lady, but she still knew her hardware business.

On June 13, 1960 we had another baby boy! Benjamin Milton Beauchemin was his name. Ben is named after my brother Ben and

Judy's father, Milton Swartzenberg. When Ben was a baby he had chubby cheeks and such a sorrowful look in his eyes. Although he was a good baby, as he grew up he sure could be stubborn at times.

Blinded by the increased and extra income, we had moved into more expensive housing, because we now had two more kids, Scott and Ben. I almost quit Sarah again, but my Area Manager gave me a subsidy income support plan and a lateral promotion to take over the Albany, NY branch territory. I had to go to Albany alone and stay in a hotel there until I found a place for us to live. When I got there, I was by myself and had to start from scratch and build a branch. We moved to Castleton, seven miles south of Albany.

I remember an incident that happened with Ben when we lived in Castleton and he was only just about a year old. Judy had tied him to a clothesline leash and left him to play by himself in the yard. Suddenly Judy looked out and saw a big, black man who had parked on the side of the road, come rushing toward Ben who was lying very still in the yard. Judy ran out there in an angry, defensive, protective manner. But, it happened that Ben had fallen asleep on the ground and was all tangled up in his rope leash. The black man saw Ben lying there and he thought that Ben was hanging himself on the rope and he was rushing to help him, contrary to what Judy thought he was doing. She thanked him and all was well again.

I set up an office in downtown Albany. I recruited and did personal sales to justify my subsidy and built a branch volume of over $1,000 a week. During this time I collected over 30 sales kits that had been abandoned in the field territory, which had a value of over $15,000 to the company. I also was assigned to build up the Schenectady branch, which I also accomplished. This was at the end of my time on subsidy. The area Manager came into my office and gave my territory to another manager from Schenectady, I think probably trying to qualify me for a Region Manager's job. I would get credit for his sales. I didn't like working for that Area Manager and I was also becoming a little disillusioned with direct sales. I decided to quit and get away from the city life and move back home to Victor. My good friend, Park drove the truck and helped me move to Victor. We rented from Judy's Mother until I could get a job and find us an apartment to rent.

I got a job as bakery route salesman for Van's Bakery out of the Perinton-Fairport office. We moved to a small two bedroom apartment on Victor's Main Street. I did well in the route sales job, making outstanding sales and earning a good income. But, after a couple of years problems arose. The bakery didn't fill my order of a special birthday cake for one of my customers. It was the same customer that it happened to three times in a row. I saw my integrity ruined. I brought the truck full of bake goods back to the bakery, turned in my keys and cash collections and then promptly quit. The boss tried to convince me to reconsider, but I was too proud to do it.

A few months later a Sarah Coventry manager friend offered me a job as Branch Manager for the Hornell/Corning branch territory. I accepted it on a subsidized basis and moved my family to Canisteo, NY. All was going well. I was trying very hard to be a success in a Sarah career, and I would work hard for it.

In Canisteo Judy blessed me with another child. It was a boy! He was born on February 20, 1963. The way he got his first name is interesting. The other kids liked to watch "Lassie" on TV. They all decided to name him Timmy after the Tim on TV. So that was it. His cousin Leo Gates (Junior), used to like to come over and play with Tim. He nick-named him "Timmer". Tim had to find his own fit into the family of brothers.

Our babysitter and good friend, Suzy Wheaton was attending college in Corning. She lived in Canesteo. One afternoon I was giving Suzy a ride home from college. I had to go over steep, winding roads and down the mountain. As I was driving down one particularly steep and winding road, I noticed my brakes were spongee and not working effectively. I didn't want to alarm Suzy, so I didn't let her know. She commented that she thought I was driving too fast and I was, but I couldn't help it, I had no brakes! We made it home safely and both of us were glad that I controlled my car. Later, we had to replace those brakes! Suzy and I had no experience at it, but she helped me to change them. We got the brake shoes exchanged and installed just fine. Then we noticed that there was lot of grease on the inside of the wheel axle and both of us feeling very proud of our work so far, didn't want to leave that dirty grease on there, so we wiped it all off. When I took the car to a local gas station to have the brakes adjusted, the garage mechanic looked at our brake job and noticed there was no grease on the axles. He asked, "Who was it that did this brake job, anyway?" I said, "Damned if I know!"

Suzy became a very good friend and sort of a Nanny for our four kids. She got permission from her parents and she came to live with us in Plattsburgh. My previous employer from in Plattsburg (Hardy's) had wanted me to return to Plattsburgh and work for him again. I took the offer. I had to go on ahead as part of the offer, so that I could start work right away. I drove to Plattsburgh that day. Then after I got there and I tried to contact Judy at our Canesteo home, I was told that Judy packed everything up and took the kids and moved to Victor to live with her mother.

I began to work that same day. The first week back in Plattsburgh I spent ten hours a day, for seven days, as a salesman at our store display at the Clinton County Fair, in Morrisonville, NY. The next Monday, Lester Hardy spoke to me about my pay arrangements. I assumed that he would pay me at least the same amount that I was making when I worked for him before, which was $80 a week. He said he always wanted to have an outside salesman on commission, but he knew that I had to have a certain amount of base salary, which he said would be only $60 per week, plus 10% commission on all my sales. I was stunned, knowing that would not give me enough income to pay my rent and to live on. I knew I was at fault for coming all that way without establishing a specific wage. I phoned Judy in Victor and told her my plight. I asked her to ask Suzy to take care of our kids for awhile, so she could come up to get a job to help out until I could get established again. Thankfully, we were able to get an apartment in the Federal Housing Project again, at a rent based on my salary. Judy came and got a job in a department store and made more money than I did. Her help was a lifesaver. Suzy was great and took care of our kids at Judy's Mother's house until we could bring them up with us.

I worked for Hardy's for three years (1963-1966). I liked working for them, especially the retail part of that business. Then for the next two years (1966-1968) I worked at Lee Appliance Store starting as Bookkeeper, Salesman and Store Manager, changing jobs for increased pay. I learned to design Wood Mode Custom Kitchens and made $300 commission on my first sale.

In Plattsburgh we had our last child, Tammy Lee Beauchemin. She was born on October 5, 1965. As a baby she had the most beautiful dark eyes. Her hair was as black as a raven's hue. I have always thought of her as my baby and she was good medicine for me.

While still at Hardy's I took a Dale Carnegie course, class #7 (1965) and joined the Plattsburgh Jaycees (1965 -1969). In 1966 I completed a diploma course in Small Business Management. In 1964 and 1968 I served as a team captain for local Community Fund drives. Then, in 1968 I received one of the Jaycee's "Outstanding Young Man of America" awards. My life's resume was published in their yearbook. I was nominated and ran for President of the local Plattsburgh Jaycee chapter, but I lost the election. I was given a plaque for my outstanding community service in the leadership roles that I held. At the installation banquet for new officers I received the plaque mentioned above and received a 15 minute standing ovation by my Plattsburgh Jaycee peer members.

While working in Plattsburgh those last years we had finally advanced ourselves financially to where we bought our first property, a beautiful home and land in Cadyville, NY. The Lord had His ways to set things up for our benefit even though we didn't know then. The next following few years in my life, through traumas, financial struggles and soul searching proved to me examples of His ways. The rewards that come out of His testing have been unbelievable benefits to those of faith. We thank you Lord for your blessings and protective love.

As a sideline for extra income, I started and ran a small business called Joe Beauchemin Enterprises, buying and selling merchandise. One item was a shapely glass bowl with an artificial rose with rose scent. It was used as a room deodorizer. I made $80 to $100 on a weekend selling them wholesale by the dozen. Finally I sold that business to my replacement Sarah Coventry branch manager. As a successful Branch Manager of Plattsburgh, I was recognized for outstanding sales and recruiting. My VP, Dick O'Donnell offered me a promotion in 1969 to take over the management of Sarah Coventry's Albany Kit Depot, at a good salary and benefits. It meant having to move to the Albany area. I accepted!

CHAPTER THIRTEEN

KIT DEPOT MANAGER

1969 – 1971

In 1969 I was promoted to the position of Zone A & M Albany Kit Depot Manager for Sarah Coventry, Inc. Jewelry sales kits were stored in inventory at the depot. As they were ordered, they were shipped to the respective field manager. The depot controlled the shipment according to the Vice-President's allotment assignments. When kits were no longer used, or they needed refurbishing, they were returned to the depot, refurbished and held in inventory again at the depot. There were over 8,000 kits (4 million dollar value) in zones A & M. I was responsible for accounting for their location at all times. The accounting system in use when I first arrived was cumbersome, inaccurate, and impossible to keep updated. I refused to use it and created a new system.

It was a mess when I first came in to start working, I was shocked and couldn't believe my eyes. Sales kits were piled high on the floor, most not refurbished and they were scattered all over the room. The records and paperwork were piled on tables and some were even on the floor. There were no staff workers, managers, or others to do this work. I was alone and reported to the Zone Depot Coordinator. Our Director was Ralph Capone, who was staff assistant to Mansell Cooke, VP.

No one could use the accounting system that was in use. It was completely useless. By using a thirteen column accounting sheet I created a system for keeping tract of the location or movement of all the kits, using a simple code that I established. Each kit had an individual number stamped on the bottom. With my system every week I could audit the depot and advise all the V.P.'s of their in-use status and account for all 8,000 kits.

I made many changes in the physical layout of the Depot work flow and changed the work stations for refurbishing kits to make it simpler for a new person to learn. The challenge I had was that I had a four hour drive to get to work and back from Plattsburgh to Albany. I would stay in a motel during the week and then drove back on Friday night. I interviewed an assistant manager and some refurbishers to get the work going. One of the key people I hired was a boy named Tripp to do inventory and jewelry assignment. He was effective and fast. I hired Jim Hoteling to be my assistant manager to work with me. We worked well together and one of our challenges was to account for the 8,000 kits every week.

A humorous thing happened to us one weekend. A tailpipe in my car burst in two and we had to figure out how to get back home. We were taking a first Aide course at the time and I decided to put a splint on the tailpipe to make it last. We stuck a tree branch in the tailpipe, and put the two end pieces together to keep it off the ground and hung it above the ground. It was alright until the wood burned up but we managed to get home before that.

I took pictures of all the changes I had made in the depot to send back to the home office for approval after I did it. I had to do all the physical moving of equipment and such all by myself. I had set it up for efficiency. Then we were ready to get going. I hired some real good refurbishers, one was my wife Judy and the other one was Judy Bishop. I also sent to the Field Vice Presidents in both zones a record of what each manager's kit status was and how many they had. The home office was impressed by all I had done and sent out an auditor to verify all that I told them. When the auditor came he couldn't believe how accurate I was and how fast I prepared and came up with the figures for the audit. He was amazed also, at how accurate my system was and was impressed at how I kept track of the location of each kit.

A bad incident happened to me one day while we were packing up issues of jewelry for shipment. I had a mini stroke. My feet felt like they were glued to the floor. I didn't pass out but my assistant made me go to the hospital. The doctors said I had a TIA which is a Transient Ischemic Attack and it had scared the tar out of everyone. I returned to work later that day.

CHAPTER FOURTEEN
OPEN HEART SURGERY

1971 – 1972

In 1971, while working at the depot, I became terribly short of breath. That coming weekend I had x-rays taken that showed a little congestion. I thought it was only a cold in my chest. It developed into Congestive Heart Failure. I was between the sale of my Cadyville home and the buying of a new house in Scotia. The doctor was treating me with a strict diet and potassium, trying to hold off an operation until I could move and be admitted into Albany Medical Center. While driving home from work one weekend, I began to experience a severe shortness of breath with even the slightest exertion. I managed to drive the four hours from Albany to Cadyville to get home but I had to stop at every rest area along the way to rest up and control my breathing. When I got home I was completely exhausted and rushed to get lying down in bed. That night I asked Judy to intervene and take control because I knew, unless she stopped me, that on Monday morning I would stupidly drive back to the Albany depot to work. I told her that I was very sick and needed her to take charge and keep me from going. She took me directly to the Emergency Room at the Plattsburgh hospital. I was hospitalized for a week or so until I had stabilized and was prepared for open heart surgery at the Burlington, Vermont Medical Center. My friend Scott Jones drove Judy and I to Burlington hospital in my Comet (my Mercury car). When we got to the hospital I was extremely weak and although I tried to be 'macho', I had to accept a ride to my room in a wheelchair. There were lots of tests and evaluations that the doctors still had to do on me. So Judy and Scott left to go back home to Cadyville.

Doctor's asked me how I got to the hospital. I said "In my comet." They looked at me strangely. I was getting ready for bed and I experienced excruciating pain in my chest. My heart valve had stopped working. Before the doctors were able to operate, another group of tests had to be completed. All night long I underwent one test or another. I remember the Heart Catherization…I was awake and watched the procedure on a TV screen. The catheter probe looked like a moving black hair. When it was inserted into my aortic heart valve, I experienced a sudden heat flash, like I never had before or since. Exhausted, I just couldn't take any more testing and I just wanted to close my eyes and die! I thought I was really talking to my wife and I really thought I was dying and said lots of things to her. I didn't know that the one I was talking to was not Judy. I talked and rambled on about our lives and our love for each other. It was a young student nurse who was very empathetic, comforting, and a good listener. She helped to comfort me throughout the night. A couple of days later after the surgery that young student nurse came to find me. She told me that she was the person I was talking to. I thanked her for her compassion and for letting me talk to her. I told her that I thought she would become a very good nurse.

The next thing I remember was being wheeled down the hall to the operating room. I remember seeing my Mom and Dad, Judy's Mom, and Judy, wishing me well and letting me know that they were praying for me. I felt as if God was riding on the cart with me. So, if God was for me, I knew nothing could be against me. I had faith and Christ's Peace to comfort me. But I knew that the next few hours would be very stressful for Judy and my family. My prayers were with them also.

During the operation that took four hours, I remember seeming to be being suspended above the operating table, looking down at myself and the medical people and feeling as if my spirit had been let loose. I thought I had died. I can recall seeing a tremendously bright light, and being compelled by it to want to go to it. I had never had an experience like that before. There was a doctor with a clipboard and during the operation he bent over me and said, "I'll have to ask Joe if he remembers me, after the operation." I did recognize and remember him!

The surgeon who operated on me was named Dr. Coffin. He told Judy that he had to use four times the amount of Morphine than for the normal heart surgery. Because of my congestive heart failure and the aortic heart valve problem, he did not want me to get completely "out" he wanted me in a state where I could respond to him and talk to him during surgery.

When I awoke, the first thing I noticed was a lot of wires connected to me and then that long incision scar running from my neck to my mid-section. It appeared that the wound had been cauterized instead of stitched. I couldn't believe I could still be alive after a cut like that and my chest spliced open. I didn't know then, about having received four times the morphine. There was no pain at all and I thought I must have died.

After I did a lot of walking in the ward and hall, I was amazed how much better I was now able to breathe when under exertion. I couldn't stop talking about the comparison to before the surgery. I was very emotional. I had all my family who were visiting me, talk with me in the ward lounge. I was so emotionally charged up and wanted to share everything with them. I told my family about the bright light, my out-of-body experience and my feeling about having received only "half a heaven." I told them how before the surgery I had been prepared for dying, if that was God's will. Because of the incidents or what ever it was, during the operation I became intently conscious of how peaceful and happy a place I had been in (I thought it was heaven). Then, waking up and still being in the hospital, seemed to me like I only got half-a-heaven. After that, most of them were too emotionally drained to stay and hear more. They said good-night and left.

I was lying in bed in my room. I was in my pajama's reading a book about the burial of fallen soldiers at Gettysburg and the work of marking their graves with white crosses. My pajama's had white crosses as a design on them. I was having a hallucination because of all the Morphine and those crosses on my pajamas started it off. There was a cleaning lady working in my room. I asked her to give me a bottle of oxygen so I could breathe well enough to finish working on putting up those white crosses on the rest of the graves. She thought I was nutty and she was right. She was frightened and left the room in a hurry. Before being discharged a psychiatrist did an EEG (Electroencephalogram) on me. It involved putting many electrodes around my skull to graph my brain waves. I guess my brain waved alright because I was finally ready to be discharged from Burlington, VT this time and went home to Cadyville.

After getting home my mother talked Judy into going grocery shopping that afternoon. They left me alone with five kids. All was well. I was just resting and watching TV. Then Scott came rushing in, in a panic, to tell me that Ben had eaten some rock salt. I called the doctor to ask if it was harmful and what should I do? I was very upset. When Judy returned she checked with the doctor who had her bring me in to his office for a check-up.

I must have had another hallucination spell because on the way to Dr. Robbin's office, I was thinking we were going on a honeymoon.

Also, while we were getting gas, our son Scott talked to us and I wondered who that kid was? Judy managed to drive us to the doctor's office. While the doctor was examining me I went into an uncontrollable rage over the fact that Dr. Robbins was not a Catholic. (Why? I have no idea.) He had to give me a sedative to get me under control and then had an ambulance bring me to the Physician's Hospital in Plattsburgh to spend a night in a padded, locked mental unit room. Reverend Klob and his wife spent the whole night ministering to me. I talked unceasingly all night. I don't remember a thing I said, but I know they were things I wouldn't have said to a minister and a lady. The next morning I was being sent back to Burlington Hospital because Dr. Robbins couldn't handle my problem. Very early in the morning I shaved and showered and got dressed. I felt and acted completely normal. In the ambulance riding over to Burlington I was smiling and joking with the ambulance staff. When I arrived at Burlington from Plattsburgh I felt normal. But, when the heart doctor there examined me he said, "So you've been having some hallucinations?" I told him, "No!" He got very upset for some reason. I was brought back up to my old bed rather than a mental ward room; maybe it would calm me? I was fearful and depressed. I retreated and became withdrawn into a comatose state, not responsive to outside stimuli. Doctors gave me electro-shock treatments. Once Judy wanted to put my slippers on me and couldn't find them. I told her that the tall doctor threw my slippers into the corner of the electric-shock room. She thought it couldn't be, until later that was where they were found. I remained in the hospital until I got over the affects of the Morphine, didn't have more hallucinations, and my behavior was back to normal.

So, I was finally ready to be discharged for the second, time under the condition that I go directly to Albany Medical Center and stay one night in the mental ward because there were no other beds available. I personally believe it was because doctors wanted to be sure that I would maintain a normal behavior with no more hallucinations.

So there we were (Joe, Judy, Eunice), standing in front of the door to the mental ward and looking in through the window in the door.

We all agreed that it looked scary inside and none of us wanted to stay there overnight. No matter, I gave my word that I would do it, so I said good-bye to Judy and Eunice and went inside.

The first thing I encountered was a couple of female inmates roaming the ward. They giggled and then acknowledged me in what was supposed to be a welcome, I think. Next, a large man in a sports coat who had a very thick black beard came in. He introduced himself as the Psychiatrist and head doctor of the mental health unit. He took me down the hall to my room. He was very nice (I wish I could remember his name). He explained why the room didn't have a door with a lock nor furniture of any kind. A mattress on the floor was my bed. Some of the inmates are very violent when they first come into the unit. The door and furniture were safety measures for all the inmates of the unit. His explanations didn't quell my fears and anxieties. He left there saying that he would come find me first thing the next morning after breakfast to take me upstairs to a better unit and room. He wished me good night and it was very hard to settle down and sleep. The room and unit were extremely dark and eerie. The only noise was coming from the sleeping patient inmates.

It was obvious that all the real psycho patients were on that ward. Across the hall was a black man who had gone berserk and wrecked his church building. In the middle of the night the black man came silently into my room. He beseeched me not to be afraid of him; that he meant me no harm. We talked (or rather he talked and I listened.) He had been a pastor of a Baptist church and one day for no apparent reason he became very violent and wrecked his church and he was confined on the unit for observation. He could see my anxiety and he came in to pray with and for me. He took good care to see I was not hurt. He scared me to death by his constant attention. In the morning he showed me the procedure for getting breakfast and in the morning's light he was no longer scary to me. I thanked him and wished him well. In the morning there were all types of mentally ill people all around me there at breakfast. They actually took care of each other, I realized and tried to be sociable while I was waiting for the doctor to come.

Shortly after, the Psychiatrist came to bring me upstairs to the better conditions. Everything was like a new world up there. I wanted to climb into bed for some good sleep to make up for staying awake most of the night before. But, I took time to observe and familiarize myself with new surroundings. It was actually a part of the mental health unit for non-violent patients (depression, etc). At first I was going to complain. Then I became more acutely aware of our unit's nurses. They all dressed in street clothes instead of uniforms. I also couldn't help but notice the short length of their skirts (probably the latest style). I could readily see the therapeutic value of their skirt length. We patients particularly enjoyed watching them make the beds. I had time and quiet to write and acknowledge my thanks to all for the cards and well wishes I received.

While I was in this hospital Reverend and Mrs. Klob ministered to me and were regular visitors. Their presence was always appreciated. They had to drive 200 miles to see me.

One day, the psychiatrist met with me. He asked all kinds of questions on many subjects in and about my life. We discussed many things. He asked what problems I thought I might have regarding my marriage and any sexual performance fears, ect., after I got home. I thought about it very carefully. My only hang-up was being in there! He complimented me on how well I coped with all I had been through and expressed admiration for my courage through it all. His appraisal and comments I really appreciated. It raised and stabilized my self-esteem and confidence. After that he discharged me from Albany Medial Center to go home to my family in Scotia, NY.

I went home to our new home in Scotia, on Glen Avenue. Seeing my children and other family members and friends again was great. All the talking and visiting exhausted me after only a few hours. I was in need of a rest and I went to bed and slept like a log.

I had been out of work and on Long-term Disability. While I was out, Sarah Coventry hired Mary Marts (wife of my past Sarah Coventry Manager). She agreed to manage the Depot in my place until I recovered and then she would turn back the responsibility to me. I appreciated all that she and Charlie did for me and for Sarah Coventry. They will always have my thanks and gratitude.

CHAPTER FIFTEEN

RECOVERY (PROMOTION)

1972 - 1973

My full recovery from Open Heart Surgery in 1972 took several months and would have occurred sooner, except for the negligence of the local pharmacist. One morning I noticed that I had passed a lot of blood in my urine. Judy took me to the doctor, who looked up the color of the Coumadin pill from the recent prescription I had taken. It turned out to be 25 mgs instead of 2.5 mgs, 10 times what it should have been. I was hospitalized again while they controlled the bleeding. Then I had to undergo an operation to probe with a camera up into my bladder to verify that there wasn't a tumor causing the bleeding, and not the Coumadin. I was in the hospital for a week. Judy and I talked about what action we should take concerning the druggist. We had already been through so much, that all we wanted was my recovery and peace, so we didn't sue him. He gave me a check for $300 as his idea of a fair compensation for what he put me through. The check bounced twice when I tried to cash it. Thirty days later he gave me cash for the $300.

Our Sarah Coventry hospital insurance was excellent, but the amount of our portion of the hospital bills was overwhelming and straining our budget. We needed help! We got it through the Catholic Charities. With their help we were able to survive, keep up our house payments, meet our obligations of our monthly bills, and not have to declare bankruptcy. We were able to keep our dignity as well. Thank God for this organization.

There was a nice city park about a mile away from our house. I walked to and back from that park faithfully every day to build up my strength and endurance. I gradually got back to normal. I went back to work at the depot gradually, working only part-time at first, then afterward I resumed the management of the Kit Depot from Mary Marts and was back into my career again.

The Sarah Coventry Albany Kit Depot was about five miles east of our home in Scotia. Judy worked as a Refurbishing Clerk in the depot and we rode together into work and back home everyday, which was very nice for us. My assistant manager was Jim Hoteling, from Schenectady. Another key person (one of my first employees) was a very creative and responsible young man from Loudonville, named Tripp Bishop. Tripp's Aunt Julie, a lady about 65+ was a very loyal helper and brought a serene effect to our work area.

An incident that happened at the depot was that everyday we found pieces of jewelry in the paper trash containers. No one could believe that one of the depot staff was a thief. The thief was the UPS man.

One humorous event happened to Jim and I. We were very busy shipping orders and Jim and I were joking around. He floored me with his joke. He said he was "busier than a one armed paper hanger with the hives." We worked well as a team.

My plus or minus kit inventory accounting system was used with individual IBM card files with kit numbers for each one. My revised reporting system for field managers advised them of their kit inventory allotment status. We had an efficient depot staff, managed by a helpful Assistant Manager. My A-M Albany Kit Depot was the most successful, efficient, least costly Depot operation of Sarah Coventry's seven operating depots within the U.S.

Then one day I got a call from the Vice President stating that he wanted me to come to the Newark home office. When I got there he gave me a promotion to become the Zone Depot Coordinator over the other seven depots around the United States. I had to relocate to Newark, New York. As a result, on November 30, 1973, I was promoted to assume the position of Kit Depot Coordinator for Sarah Coventry's seven depot operations. Their locations were:

Albany, NY.
Zone A and M

Richmond, VA.
Zone B

Atlanta, GA .
Zone C

Butler, PA .
Zone D

Des Moines, IA .
Zone E

Dallas, TX .
Zone F

Freemont, CA .
Zone G

My Vice-President was Mansell Cooke. My manager was Ralph Capone, Director of Kit Depots at Sarah Coventry Inc. Newark, New York State.

This job meant having to move closer to Newark, NY to be able to work out of the Newark home office. We moved to Judy's mother's house temporarily until we bought a house in Macedon and had closed on it.

When the field managers from the Sarah Coventry sales group that I used to work with, heard that I had been promoted and was going to the Newark office to work they put on a surprise lunch celebration to honor me and Judy, who also was leaving her work at the depot. I almost discovered what they were doing, because one of the managers came in on some pretext. I wondered why she was at the depot, but I still never suspected anything. It was a very nice gesture and we had a good time together at lunch.

In the beginning I drove to work every day from Victor. I was pleasantly surprised on my first day to find that I had a reserved parking space in front of the main Sarah Coventry building with my name printed on the pavement. That was a nice benefit to help me recover quickly from my surgery. I wouldn't have to walk the long way from the employee parking lot. That was considerate. I'm sure it was some of Mansell's doing. He was like that!

In the home office building I had a very nice office, right next to Ralph Capone, Department Director. It had a glass wall that allowed me to look out at the department staff and also see out to the outside through the other window facing a courtyard that had a tree and a fountain. It was exceptional working conditions.

This was a dream come true to me. Ever since way back in 1958-59 when I first had contact or knowledge of Sarah Coventry, I had dreamed about being a part of this company in a salaried management role like this one, that would give me the opportunity to prove my value and have the potential to earn a good life for myself and family. I vowed then that I would make an outstanding profitable mark for Sarah Coventry, Inc. For fourteen years (1959-1973 = 14 years, not consecutive) as a branch manager I had sought after this Sarah Coventry dream career. I had failed several times, but I never gave up the dream. I worked as a Branch Manager for ten of those 14 years and built a branch sales group five times, Plattsburgh, Albany, Schenectady, Canesteo and Plattsburgh again. All of them are within New York State. I had paid my dues!

I had a parallel career (10 years in retail management) that became a "fall-back-on" source of steady income whenever the commission earnings got too irregular for me to be able to support my large family of five children, my wife and me.

Just one piece of experience to share with anyone reading my book that has a dream, goal, or desire to win and achieve their success: Never give up! I found out after a lot of failures and struggles in my life this "SECRET"...You are never a failure...until you give up and you quit! I had to learn a lot of new things during these times in my career. It was easier when I was younger, but enthusiasm never gets old. With the right amount of enthusiasm, a person can do anything!

CHAPTER SIXTEEN

EXECUTIVE CAREER (SUCCESS)

1973 - 1980

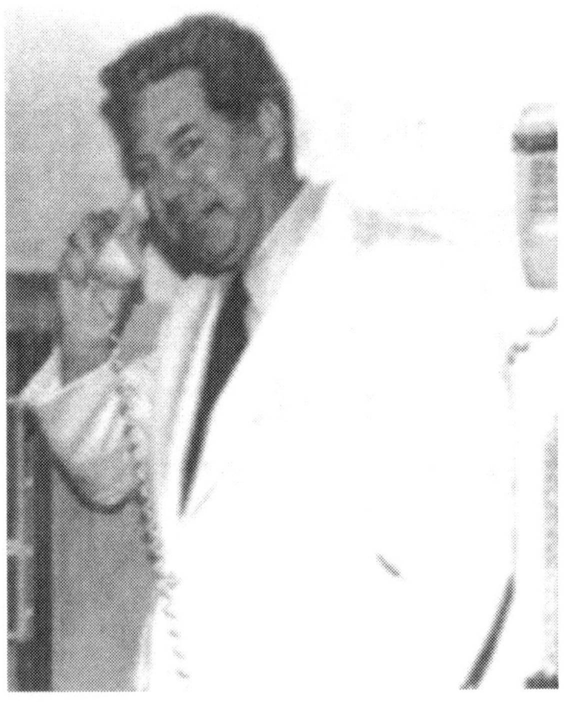

Telecommunications Manager - Director of Administration
1980

The History of Sarah Coventry, Inc. and C. H. Stuart, Inc., Parent Company in Newark, New York is recorded here in order to preserve its memory and its existence for posterity. Bill Stuart, of Newark, NY, was the owner of The Commercial Enterprises, a group of individual businesses, including Jackson & Perkins (Roses), Caroline Emmons (Jewelry), Gateway Home Distributors (Home Decorating), Hanover Distributors (Packaging-Shipping), and Corporate Audit & Accounting (Administration), all collectively known as C. H. Stuart, Inc. headquartered on Main Street in Newark, NY. Their newest company was Sarah Coventry, Inc. led by it's founder and first President, Bill Stuart. He was the first to envision Sarah's growth potential and dreamed of it's reality and the income and recognition opportunities it brought to it's people.

In 1949 Bill hired a young man named Rex Wood to take over as Sales Manager and President. With a few jewelry samples, Rex, in Holcomb, NY, demonstrated the first Sarah Coventry jewelry party. He called it a Fashion Show to the hostess and guests. It proved to him that women would buy jewelry on the home-party plan of merchandising. It was successful.

One of Sarah's assets and big reason for it's rapid growth was Al Winfrey, as Vice-President of Sales Promotion. With the influence of this leader many successful changes were made to improve the image of the company and also it's jewelry demonstrators. He named a party, a Fashion Show and therefore, demonstrators became Fashion Show Directors (FSD's). The designs and quality of Sarah's jewelry were constantly monitored to stay 'top notch', and earned the high rating of Fine Fashion Jewelry. Because of all these positive improvements, the company's image and acceptance rose in the minds of potential customers, hostesses and recruits. All sales people agreed that people bought Sarah's jewelry on their own; no one had to sell it to them. It only needed to be shown and the jewelry sold itself. Thus recruits happily became FSD's. Successful, profitable sales branches were built, and Sarah grew bigger.

Mansell Cooke, was Vice-President & General Manager of Sarah Coventry Inc. I have always admired Mansell Cooke ever since I first met him, when I was a Sarah Coventry Branch Manager. I liked his personality, strength and leadership and I have always tried to emulate him and look up to him as a mentor. He always praised and gave recognition. He saw the economy of doing shipments out of the sales zone, instead of from the Newark office. He developed a 7 Zone Depot organization in the U.S. I managed the Albany Depot until 1973. About 1975, Mansell and managers from C. H. Stuart realized that doing all service functions for all companies from one service operation, versus individually, would be a great enough savings for the corporation that a payback of cost monies invested could be achieved in a relatively short period of time. A new division was created called Corporate Services Division (CSD).

CSD did all of the maintenance of all buildings and grounds, security, repaired all office equipment, did all printing, all mail functions, provided warehousing and receiving. I was responsible for all copier equipment and supplies, administered all telephone equipment and provided usage cost control, shipping and packaging. It housed the Zone A/M Sarah Coventry Depot. When administrative needs arose, like Tour Guides, then CSD administration provided the service. CSD handled just about any kind of service needed by an individual company or by the corporation itself.

All my experience and management instinct told me that this new division was an ideal opportunity for my career advancement, and that the timing was right. I had a plan that meant risking my job if it didn't work (but an executive has to take calculated risks in order to lead). I took my job description and gave my job away, half to Ed Smalldone, and half to Walt Baker, my two manager candidates that I had been training; so I had a replacement for my job. I had in effect just given them lateral promotions. I was banking on upper management's approval. I did not have the authority to do what I did.

I sent advisory notice to Ralph Capone, my supervising manager, with a description of what I had done, and notice that I was going to talk to Mansell, too. I didn't want anyone to think that I was taking this action behind their backs, or was trying to go over their heads. Then, I sent my letter of request and my resume and credentials right away that day, to Mansell Cooke, Vice President, with a letter to him stating what I was hoping to gain from my rash, risky actions. He approved and let stand the two promotions I had made by splitting my job description. He promoted me to the position of Systems and Procedures Administrator for CSD, with a $3,000 a year raise. I asked to have a secretary, and he said, "Get one!" I asked to keep Ed Smalldone as my assistant; he approved. Further, he assigned me to an office and an area where I could set up my department. He told me to go to the warehouse and take what furniture items I would need for a department. Ed and I did as he directed, (even though the furniture was ordered for a different department).

I put a lot of hard work and devotion into my job as Systems & Procedures Administrator. My first assignment was to coordinate the move of all seven C. H. Stuart companies from Main Street to the new headquarters building. This including managing all telephone and office repair service. I also was responsible for all Personnel functions and I created and published a CSD Systems and Procedures Manual. I used all my skill and hard work in doing an excellent job. I met with Mansell regularly to discuss my progress report with him, mentioning to him that the other four managers in CSD were at Director level. He knew what I was after and he told me that I definitely had earned a lateral promotion and he made me Director of Administration & Procedures (no salary raise, but I received a nice bonus from him at the end of the year).

I was elated with all the challenges he had given me since I joined CSD. I thoroughly enjoyed my job, and especially the travel to cities that I had never been to before (all First Class). My year end progress reports to Mansell gave him a report of my goals and achievements.

CHAPTER SEVENTEEN

MAJOR DEPRESSION (LIFE AGAIN)

1980 - 1990

The kids all wanted to play too!

I continued on with CSD until the end of 1979. Personal life stresses and the close working relationship between Mansell and I had changed. He asked me what happened to me and did he do something to me? No, he hadn't done something to me...I had changed and became depressed by all the personal stress created by both my daughters getting pregnant and their putting the babies up for adoption. Then my father had a series of heart attacks and after the last one he developed Acute Leukemia and died two weeks later.

My mother had a depressive personality and was the worrier type. She was illiterate so she depended completely on my father. When he died, each of us three children tried to make a home for her at each of our homes. But her personality and support needs were more than we could handle. We had to move her in to Thompson Hospital Nursing Home in Canandaigua. She lived there for ten years. She developed a severe stomach cancer, and died at the nursing home in 1994 at 89 years of age. She was a loving wife, mother and grandmother. She is missed.

Prior to that, Judy's mother, Eunice Swartzenberg, developed severe complications from her breast cancer. I drove her to Rochester for treatments. It was hard to be there watching her bravely fight the cancer. She was the best Mother-in-law that any man could have. I loved her as a mother. I know that she cared for me too. She died in 1983, at 76 years of age, in Thompson Hospital Nursing Home in Canandaigua. She too is missed.

So all those stresses and heartaches finally got to me and gave me an Angina attack at work in December of 1979. When I recovered, I went to Rochester General Hospital to determine if I had Coronary Heart Disease. Doctors said that I did not. They put their diagnosis in writing in a letter to me and I brought the letter to Vice President, Mansell. He felt that he must reduce my responsibilities and work load because of the changes in my health. That was "the straw that broke the camel's back." I felt I had been knocked off my role as a successful leader in the business. I became very withdrawn from my peers and management. I started experiencing fear and anxiety and loss of my self-esteem. I reasoned that at age 46, with a medical and physical history like mine, and a large family of five kids to support, I was never going to be able to get executive work again and fell into a big pit of despair and depression. I went into the Clifton Springs Hospital Mental Health Clinic for treatment of Depression.

One day at home I was especially weary of all this depression, etc. and I took a bunch of Lithium capsules to sleep and rest my mind. I don't think I wanted to try to commit suicide. I was just at the end of my endurance. My son Ben found me on the bed that afternoon and made me wake up. I was brought to the "R" wing of Strong's Mental Health Unit in Rochester. I felt like I was trapped in a deep, dark pit. No matter how much I tried I couldn't climb out. At first I was in the Day Care program at Strong Memorial Hospital, but having to drive there and back under heavy medication and in heavy traffic was more than I could cope with. I started feeling like I could get control of my depression. I would climb up and almost over the top, then I would fall back in again. Dr. Wells tried different medicines and put me on the Research Department's list, looking for a new medicine that would help me. In the meantime, I received many, many electric shock treatments which helped some for short periods of time. Finally the research people suggested larger doses of Lithium, along with a new drug called Prozac. It started to help. I could concentrate and read again. I joined the outside physical therapy games, and also did some nice craft projects and befriended an older man and helped him.

One day I said to Dr. Wells. "I heard that the Rochester Museum was hiring volunteers." I went there and was hired as a volunteer. With this progress I was shortly discharged from the hospital and went home. I worked at the museum until late fall. Then I went to work at K-mart as a part time stock clerk, and later went full time. I became the Lead Clerk and received awards for Customer Service and once was chosen as the "Employee of the Month".

I resigned from K-mart once, to take a job as Assistant Manager of Penser's Diversified Services, in Palmyra NY. It lasted for one year and then, because of low finances, I was laid off. The work was typesetting and preparing the Timesaver weekly paper. I went to

New York City to attend training in the use of the IBM computers for typesetting. Also, I was hired to set up a telephone line and modem for customer access on the line to Penser's transmitting data that needed to be typeset. I accomplished these goals before I was laid off. Then I drew unemployment for the first time in my life.

I enrolled and completed a course in Electronics at BOCES in Flint. I did well but decided it wasn't the work that I wanted to do in my life. I returned to work at K-Mart in the Perinton store.

We sold our residence home in Farmington (Macedon) for $90,000 and netted $60,000 after expenses, because of 15 years of appreciation. We bought a 3 bedroom log cabin, with a full walk out cellar, a pond, and 7.5 acres of land with a beautiful view, in Branchport NY for $60,000 cash.

After that I still worked at K-Mart and drove to and from work. I had trouble staying awake while driving, so I decided to quit driving to be safe. At this time, I was receiving almost $1,000 a month from my rental investments alone so I decided to retire from K-Mart (no monies received), to stay at the cabin and worked on it during the day. We still hadn't closed and moved from the Macedon house yet. Then one morning about 3 a.m. we got a phone call from our tenant in Cohocton saying that our rental house was on fire. It was a total loss. That was in February 1990. We moved to our cabin home on December 31, 1990. We received $70,000 insurance settlement for the house, a $65,000 profit return in 5 years. That turned out to be a good investment. The several real estate transactions made me more aware of the amount of equity value that we would gain from selling our Macedon home. We had enough to buy with cash and have no mortgage payments. From our real estate investments we made a total of $115,000 profit in 13 years

I used some of the profits to fix up our log cabin, since I had retired from K-Mart. It took me two years working alone to get the cabin caulked and painted and other improvements made.

Let me describe this cabin: The cabin's size is about 25' x 50'. It has a barn shaped roof line that allows room for a second story, with two bedrooms and an open stairway. The first floor has one bedroom, a bathroom, kitchen, hall, and a 25' x 25' large living room with cathedral ceiling, about 20 ft high and a ceiling fan. Half of the living area is used as a formal dining room. It is separated from the open Wood Mode kitchen by a sit-down counter/bar. There is a full cellar, with concrete floor and walls, one extra block high for easy walking. There is a door to access the outside back yard. As for heating, the cabin has baseboard electric heat in every room, plus a great cast iron wood stove that will easily heat the whole cabin very toasty by itself.

I continually worked on updating the cabin. We replaced all carpets and tile floors. Replaced all windows and storm doors. Updated and corrected all Plumbing and electrical problems and repaired the Septic tank. I used my three-pound hammer to demolish all unused out buildings and cleaned up the debris. For most of two years I caulked between the logs of the cabin and then painted the whole cabin by myself.

CHAPTER EIGHTEEN

THE STROKE AND SEIZURES

1992 - 1996

After release from stroke center

I discovered that there are two types of strokes, a thrombolic stroke that occurs when a blood clot blocks a cerebral artery in the brain and a hemorrhagic stroke occurs when a blood vessel in the brain ruptures.

One morning in February of 1992, I was sitting on my couch in the living room of my log cabin home on Italy Friend Road and was trying to tie the laces in my boots, getting ready to go outside to work on the cabin. I became aware that I couldn't feel the boot laces on my fingers and I started to become alarmed. Suddenly all my muscles went limp and I fell off the couch and landed on the floor. There was no pain, but the shock reaction was disturbing to me physically, mentally, and emotionally. It took me a few minutes to grasp what was happening to me. It was eerie quiet in the cabin. I was alone. Judy had gone to work at Clifton Springs Hospital. My nearest phone was a wall phone some 25 feet away across the room. You can bet that I was plenty worried. I didn't know if I would die, so I prayed to Jesus for His peace and help for comfort and inspiration for what to do next. I thought of my mother and how she once told me about a similar time when she also had to crawl to get help in her situation. My bladder and my colon were fighting to lose control but thankfully I didn't have an 'accident'. I prayed for help and determination and I crawled across the floor. My first priority was the toilet. How I managed to climb up on it and stay on it is beyond me. Then I crawled over to the phone and pulled it down off the hook. A man operator was on the line. I told him I was having a stroke and needed help. He got information from me about my name and location and directions to get to my house. He said that he had called an ambulance, but they had gotten on the wrong road and were lost and delayed. So all that I could do was to lie on the floor, pray and wait. He connected me with Judy and the ambulance on a conference call where we could all talk and hear each other. I tried to stay calm and tell jokes. Actually I was losing mental control and having hallucinations.

Finally the ambulance arrived and they took me directly to Soldiers and Sailors Hospital in Penn Yan. My stroke happened at about 10 am but it was about 1 pm when the ambulance arrived. You bet I was I glad to see them! Now, even after 6 years of extensive therapy I can not crawl across those 25 feet. How I did it then I don't know. Up where I live, it seems that everything is called Italy something or something Friend. The ambulance driver came up the wrong road and it took time to figure out where I was. I was lucky that they did find me.

They took me to Soldiers and Sailors Hospital in Penn Yan but they couldn't treat me there so I was taken to Clifton Springs Hospital. I stayed there until I could be transported to the Stroke Unit at Strong Memorial Hospital in Rochester. I think My family believed that I might die. The effects of the stroke were causing me to talk a lot and tell what I thought were humorous stories. That upset Judy. The doctor told her that it was quite typical with stroke victims. My reason for telling stories was only for me to relieve the stress and tension of the situation. I remember naming my nurse Sue-Joe after she came into my room and said "Hi, my name is Sue, Joe", and it stuck.

At Clifton Springs I received extensive physical therapy and occupational therapy for about two weeks. After this I was still in bad shape and was transported to Rochester to Strong's Stroke Rehab Unit. It was there that I first became aware how bad off I really was. When it finally sunk in that I was paralyzed it was a scary and depressing feeling. It took me awhile to accept and learn to use the wheelchair. I kept trying to get out of bed to use the toilet and I'd end up sprawled on the floor. Finally nurses attached an alarm to my leg so they would know when I was trying to get out of bed. Then gradually it came time to learn to walk. This was frightening at first; then challenging! I learned to use a cane and walk by myself. The scariest time was learning to go down stairs…using my weak leg first. That was one time that tested my courage and faith.

In Occupational Therapy I worked on my stroke and clubbed left hand, I saw miracles happen as it gradually came "alive". I prayed a lot for the "Peace of Christ" to strengthen me to accept what I could not change and to be willing to give myself over to His care and not to give up.

I came home from Strong Hospital in a wheelchair. Doctor's told Judy that I may never walk again, before I would be released to go home. She was told to have a ramp entrance put on our house and other physical changes inside the house to accommodate a wheelchair. I used the wheelchair for about a week and then I abandoned it and used a brace and cane to walk by myself.

I was tested and passed to get my driver's license. After a while it became obvious that it was unsafe for me to drive so I surrendered my license. I never realized how depressing life would be after I gave up driving. It has been a long hard fourteen years since my stroke. The biggest benefit that came out of the stroke was, and I praise God, that I don't smoke anymore. I have learned to appreciate the many blessings I have received more that I ever could have before. After fourteen years of therapy, I still can no longer walk even with a cane. I have to use a walker. I go all over and stay active using the walker.

My left hand has improved greatly. My goal was to play my guitar once again. I know now that I never will. I have learned how to cope better with life and I have gotten my depression somewhat under control.

Once, after doing some heavy work and getting very tired, I suddenly developed a seizure disorder in my left hand an arm. My hand and arm started to jerk wildly. My neck was twisted to one side and my eyes were being pulled to the same side. It was not terribly painful but it was scary. It only lasted for three to five minutes. My doctor called it a focal seizure, not as serious as the Grand Mall type. Whenever my Dilantin medicine level is not adequate, I then have one or two seizures. In response, I just get as comfortable and as safe as possible and as relaxed as I can. After the seizure I am very tired and must rest for an hour or so, taking a short nap helps a lot. I keep as active as possible. The scariest seizure episode happened when I was working in my garden. I just lied down on the ground in the garden and just waited for it to stop. I can vacuum, help with the laundry and dishes. For enjoyment, I work on crafts, take walks around my yard and watch videos.

I was making good progress, then just after Christmas (1997), I tipped over in a chair at the dining room table. I went over backwards and struck my neck and shoulders on the edge of the countertop with a loud smack! Everyone was shocked. My son Ben right away came to check me out and comfort me. At the time I felt that I was fine, but then I started having pains in my arm and shoulder. My doctor gave me a shot of Cortisone. Later the Orthopedic specialist diagnosed it as Impingement of the Shoulder.

CHAPTER NINETEEN

CONTINUED ADVERSITIES

1997 - 2006

One night I was having a restless time trying to get to sleep. I rolled over too quickly and fell out of bed. I landed on the pointed corner of the night stand. It hit me on the inside of my ear and nearly ripped my left ear off. It bled profusely. No matter what I did, the bleeding would not stop. I was taken to the hospital Emergency Room. It required a Plastic Surgeon to get the bleeding stopped and stitched up. She used some type of jell made especially for treating bleeding. After she put stitches in, she bandaged my ear and wrapped white gauze around my head. I looked as if I'd been to war. She asked me "How did you cut your ear?" and my answer was, "I rolled out of bed!"

At another time, I was on Coumadin, a blood thinner that takes longer to get bleeding to stop. I had to go to the Emergency room in an ambulance to stop the bleeding from a tiny cut on my finger. A few times my lips or gums have been bleeding because of Gingivitis. I have found bleeding from anyplace on the face, bleeds more profusely. When my Dilantin level is too high it becomes toxic and make me feel like a zombie and I can't cope well but I've learned how to use my faith to psyche myself and gain self control I don't get alarmed or fearful, just stay cool and cope with things.

Falls and Hospitalizations

The bathroom has been a dangerous place for me. For instance, one day I slipped on water left on the floor and fell against the toilet bowl. At first I didn't think that I got hurt, but an x-ray showed a crack in my pelvic bone. It caused lots of pain. It took over three months for it to heal. In 2004 my right arm got tendonitis from using it to push off, rising up from a chair. My cousin Bob gates sent me money to buy a power lift chair. I am grateful because it helps me a lot. I am doing Physical Therapy at home now.

Other Difficult Adversities

In 1997, I had quadruple heart by passes. In the recovery room I was choking on the instrument that was put in my throat for breathing. I didn't know it was there. I kept trying to get it out. I got completely exhausted. I even felt that I had died. I told Judy, when she came to tell me that everything had gone fine, I said to her, "I'm sorry Judy, I died!" To do the surgery the vein in my left leg was removed to be used as bi-pass arteries. The scar runs from my groin down to my ankle on my left leg. Cellulitis with a severe high fever developed in that leg. In 1999 I spent four weeks in the hospital in critical condition for that. I have had several falls but I have used a method my Occupational Therapist taught me. I just sit down when I fall and get myself up. In 1997 I had a Colonoscopy and had four Polyps removed. Occasionally I still get Angina pains. . I am still fighting off depression attacks. I suffer with incontinence and impotence. In 2004 my heart rate became too fast and it was necessary to shock my heart to get it back to my normal rate.

On my own I started an exercise program at home; water therapy, and Physical Therapy all help. I completed Cardiac Rehab. Using a walker I go out to movies, family gatherings, and to doctor visits. I meet my friend Conrad to go out for lunch or we stay home and watch videos. I have been doing a daily exercise routine to practice walking with and without a cane or walker. I have been writing short stories and my autobiography, "Up from Adversity." These activities help me stay happy.

Emotional Losses

Josette Beauchemin Crane: 1958 - 1999, Age 41

She was our first child…to be born and to die. When Judy informed me of the tragic event I was in the hospital at the time. She said to me, "We've lost her Honey." My world came crashing in on me. Our hearts were broken. She and I had a special bond. She was truly a "little Joe". She died from a systemic infection following surgery in the colon. We miss her and think of her daily.

Suzanne Wheaton Devins: 1944 - 2005, Age 60

She was like one of our children and was a great friend. She lived in Plattsburgh, New York. She died of heart failure. Judy and Suzy were best friends for many years. We miss her semi-annual visits too.

My Philosophy

Over the years I have developed a philosophy, that is...to never accept "Quit" or "Give up". My inner force will not let me accept them or acknowledge them.

Summary

I have been blessed with kind friends and family. And I am doubly blessed to have a loyal wife who has taken a lot off my shoulders and is the best of caregivers.

To the Readers of My Book

I hope that you have found it interesting, inspiring, and enjoyable, as much as I have enjoyed writing it.

EPILOGUE

From my life history, it seems to me that I will always be plagued with one continuous hardship after another, but I am blessed to have a challenging, exciting and rewarding life.

In my life I have earned recognition, awards and relationships with many fine people and loyal friends.

Sometimes there were disappointments and even failures. Through it all, hard times and medical traumas have taught me valuable lessons that have given me a greater appreciation of the true values of life.

I had good Christian parents and the love, for 49+ years, of a wonderful loyal and compassionate wife. I have lived to be 72 years old to date, even though doctor's prediction was that I would not live to be 21. God has given me an extra 50+ years. I have always tried to make the best use of that time.

Hopefully, family and friends will enjoy this book and treasure it.

My favorite Bible quote is:

I can do all things through Christ who strengthens me! Phil. 4:13

Love and regards,
Joseph Beauchemin, Author

Printed in the United States
66059LVS00007B/10-54

9 781424 160921